POWER WRITING
Ten Steps to Success

Toby Larson
and
JE Sparks

HDL PUBLISHING COMPANY
A Division of
HDL COMMUNICATIONS
Costa Mesa, CA 92626

Power Writing—Ten Steps to Success
Toby Larson and JE Sparks

Library of Congress Cataloging-in-Publication Data
Larson, Toby, 1944-
    Power writing.

    1. Business writing.   2. English language—Business
English.   I. Sparks, J.E.   II. Title.
HF5718.3.L37   1989   808'.066651   88-32808
ISBN 0-937359-39-4

Published by
HDL Publishing
A Division of HDL Communications, Inc.
702B Randolph Avenue
Costa Mesa, California 92626
(714) 540-5775

Cover Design by Mike Dirham

10 9 8 7 6 5 4 3 2 1
Printed in the United States of America

CONTENTS

viii

ACKNOWLEDGMENTS

Special thanks to Rona Wade, for her invaluable help editing and support in putting the book together; and to Natalie Goldberg, author of *Writing Down the Bones*, for providing us with several unique ideas from her book.

INTRODUCTION

Words. They have incredible power, whether spoken or written. Often they can make the difference between the success or failure of a new proposal. Fuzzy vocabulary, and the ambiguity of meaning that often results, can cause you to lose an important account. On the other hand, carefully chosen words will immediately grab attention, will motivate and persuade.

You write business letters, memos, and reports not because you want to but because you must. A letter or memo is due explaining why sales figures have declined. Would you ask your secretary to write that memo for you? You have to evaluate a new employee relations program. Would you normally pull out a form letter from the files and duplicate it? You have to write a breakdown of your company's major projects. Would you try to use words that sound impressive, even though they don't express what you want to say? Whatever the writing task, you must get to the point as quickly as possible. Nobody else can do the job for you.

The volume of paperwork that business professionals generate on a daily basis continues to mushroom. You don't have much time to waste when writing your message, nor should you think that your client has any more time to read that message than you do to write it.

So where should you go for help? Hundreds of managers, salespeople, secretaries, and educators have followed our program and achieved success quickly. This course provides only those skills you will need today and tomorrow in business. What features does *Power Writing* have that will give you greater confidence?

☆ Ten easily mastered stages

☆ Models drawn from business letters, memos, and reports

☆ Tips for rewriting and polishing

☆ Lists of unnecessary words and phrases eliminated in order to achieve greater clarity

☆ Ways to vary your sentences to capture your reader's attention

Don't start in the middle of the book or at the back. You will get the most benefit by beginning with the easy steps. Then work your way up toward the later stages. Remember when you started your first full-time job. Obviously you didn't learn everything you needed to know on the first day. You had to take time to move through the massive amounts of data and feel comfortable about your new position. The same goes for business writing.

Writing powerfully requires discipline and persistence. You not only have to write your correspondence but edit and polish it as well. Business professionals who rise to the top of their companies communicate clearly and concisely. Good writing skills will help you to listen better, articulate more clearly, and force others to explain what they mean. In short, you will come to work with a sense of renewed confidence, ready to meet the challenges of the day. You will feel empowered to take charge of your environment.

AND NOW FOR THE PRE-TEST!

Be open to learning how to put your ideas on paper more effectively. Discard your old fears about writing. You are in a unique position to have your written work evaluated by writing professionals without the pressure of someone looking over your shoulder, ready to correct you. Before you start the program, pick up your pen and create a paragraph of no more than seven sentences.

You may choose a "how-to" approach:

☆ Sell a particular product

☆ Improve morale within your company

☆ Use networking to improve your business

OR a subjective paragraph:

☆ Recommend someone for a job

☆ Complain about a product or service

☆ Thank a client for his purchase

Mail your paragraph to us. After reviewing it, we will return it to you immediately with comments and suggestions specific to your needs.

Communication Associates
2160 Century Park East, Suite 201 North
Los Angeles, CA 90067

The measure of man is what he does with power.
(Pittacus—650?-569? B.C.)

Now, go for Power!

STAGES 1-2-3

WORD, PHRASE, AND SENTENCE POWER

(10 minutes a day)

WHAT IS POWER?

☆ The ability or capacity to act or perform effectively

WHAT IS POWER WRITING?

☆ The ability to write effective, readable material

POWER WRITING. . .

☆ Uses 1st Power for main ideas, topic sentences, topic paragraphs

☆ Uses 2nd Power for major details that explain main ideas

☆ Uses 3rd Power for minor details that elaborate upon or clarify major details

☆ Provides for expansion of thought: 4th Power explains 3rd Power, 5th Power amplifies 4th Power, and so on to successive Powers

DO YOU HAVE 10 MINUTES TO SPARE?

☆ Focus for 10 minutes on a problem you must tackle, a daydream, an idea.

☆ Pick up your favorite pen. Set it to paper. Write down only the bones of what you have been thinking about. The bare bones. Find that Power in you!

DON'T WORRY ABOUT YOUR TALENT OR CAPABILITY

☆ That will grow as you practice.

☆ Capability is like a water table below the surface of the earth. No one owns it, but you can tap into it. Tap into your own writing capability, and your own style will come through.

☆ When you learn to trust that your style of writing is your own stamp, your own mark, you are ready to direct that voice toward others. THAT'S POWER!

YOUR WEEKLY TIME PLAN

Set up a time plan for working with the 10 stages of this book. Follow the plan for 10 weeks. Then determine how you might wish to adjust the plan to achieve the mastery you want.

Week 1	Stages 1-2-3	10 minutes/day
Week 2	Stage 4	10 minutes/day
Week 3	Stage 5	20 minutes 3 times/week
Week 4	Stage 6	20 minutes 3 times/week
Week 5	Stage 7	20 minutes 3 times/week
Week 6	Stage 8	30 minutes 2 times/week
Week 7	Stage 9	30 minutes 2 times/week
Week 8	Stage 9	30 minutes 2 times/week
Week 9	Stage 10	30 minutes 2 times/week
Week 10	Stage 10	30 minutes 2 times/week

STAGE 1: WORD POWER

Words, phrases, sentences, and paragraphs all have Power as they relate to other words, phrases, sentences, and paragraphs. A 1st Power word serves as the most general word under which the 2nd Power words belong.

Start with Word Power, Stage 1 of 10 Stages, to master the concept of Power. Get very comfortable with the first three Stages. Make time for these crucial Stages, as they will prepare you for the next seven.

Study these word sets. Note that one of the words has a number (1) for 1st Power and that the others have a (2) for 2nd Power.

POWER FLOW

(1) officers
> (2) president
> (2) secretary

(1) securities
> (2) stocks
> (2) bonds

(1) professions
> (2) engineering
> (2) accounting

(1) airlines
> (2) United
> (2) American

(1) computers
        (2) Apple
        (2) IBM

(1) fuels
        (2) gasoline
        (2) coal

STAGE 1 ACTIVITY

☞ Complete the following Power Flow charts. See the Appendix for possible responses.

(1) hotels
        (2) Hilton
        (2)

(1) products
        (2)
        (2)

(1)
        (2) Washington
        (2)

(1) foods
      (2)
      (2)

(1)
      (2)
      (2) Reagan

(1) stores
      (2)
      (2) Sears

(1)
      (2) oil
      (2) gas

(1)
      (2)
      (2) England

(1)
      (2) football
      (2)

(1) corporations
      (2)
      (2)

STAGE 2: PHRASE POWER

A phrase, with two or more words, conveys one thought. Unlike a sentence, a phrase is not complete. It does not have a subject and a verb. In the following models, note how some words from Stage 1 have now become Power phrases, with 1st and 2nd Power tags.

POWER FLOW

(1) corporate officers
      (2) president
      (2) treasurer

(1) fuels for industrial use
      (2) unleaded gasoline
      (2) diesel fuel

(1) international airlines
      (2) Pan American
      (2) Trans-World

(1) financial institutions
      (2) Bank of America
      (2) Wells Fargo Bank

(1) American newspapers
      (2) *The New York Times*
      (2) *The Wall Street Journal*

STAGE 2 ACTIVITY

☞ Complete the following Power Flow charts. See the Appendix for possible responses.

(1) hotel chains
- (2) Holiday Inn
- (2) Best Western

(1) department stores
- (2) the Bay
- (2) Neiman-Marcus

(1) electronic products
- (2) Beta max VCR
- (2) Sony TV

(1) Non-renewable Resources
- (2) natural gas
- (2) natural oil

(1) American Cities
- (2) New York City
- (2) Chicago

(1) World Nations
- (2) australia
- (2) New Zealand

(1) international foods
- (2) Raw Caribou
- (2) French Fries

(1) Nat. Sports
- (2) NFL football
- (2) NHL Hockey

STAGE 3: SENTENCE POWER

A sentence has a subject and a verb. Unlike a phrase, a sentence expresses a complete thought. Just as words and phrases have Power, so do sentences in their relationships with each other. In the following models, note how some phrases in Stage 2 have now become sentences.

(1) Two corporate officers had specific tasks at the meeting.

    (2) The president conducted the session.

    (2) The treasurer made a financial report.

(1) A businessman often reads two daily newspapers.

    (2) He may read *The New York Times.*

    (2) He also may read *The Wall Street Journal.*

(1) Industry makes use of at least two fuels.

    (2) Corporate automobiles use unleaded fuel.

    (2) Company trucks use diesel fuel.

(1) Several American airlines fly international routes.

    (2) Pan American flies to Paris.

    (2) Trans-World Airlines flies to London.

STAGE 3 ACTIVITY

At this stage, your goal is to write three complete sentences in Power 1 2 2. Read the following models.

1. As the best candidate, Timothy possesses special qualities. He has top-notch communication skills. He also presents a favorable appearance.

2. Driving on the freeway, I had thoughts about the upcoming meeting. Should I bring up the matter that had bothered me for days? Should I question company policy?

3. The employees, overwhelmed with gratitude, showed their appreciation in special ways. They chipped in to buy a watch for Jim. They also autographed a large poster card.

1st POWER SENTENCES

☆ Check for sentence fragments.

fragment: because I admire Jim

  sentence: Because I admire Jim, I voted for him.

fragment: two reasons for going

  sentence: Jack had two reasons for going to the meeting.

Activities for 1st Power Sentences

☞ Make the following fragments into sentences. See the Appendix for possible responses.

  1. state-of-the-art programs

  2. at the ticket office

  3. reasons for improving my writing

  4. to write this letter of complaint

☆ Have a dictionary at hand. If you write on a word processor, use the spell checker.

☆ Use commas when in doubt. Read a sentence aloud. Put in a comma when you pause.

　　Example: If you take the coastal route, you will reach Malibu before I do.

☆ At this point, do not be concerned about neatness, margins, and indenting. Just get your ideas down.

☆ Find a personal editor. Have your writings checked by a former teacher, a close friend, a colleague—someone whose ability you trust. You need someone who has nothing to gain by protecting your feelings and nothing to lose by being honest.

☞ Twenty 1st Power sentences follow. Select seven sentences to create seven three-sentence paragraphs of 1 2 2. Copy one of the 1st Power sentences on a sheet of paper. Add two 2nd Power sentences to complete the paragraph.

　　1. (Name of company) offers employees unique benefits.

　　2. The manager made two specific requests of his staff.

　　3. What incredible luck the company had!

　　4. When the new chief executive officer arrived, the company changed in obvious ways.

　　5. Showing confidence, the treasurer presented two possible solutions to the dilemma.

6. To do the job of transporting passengers by rail better and faster, Amtrak instituted new policies.

7. Limited to two choices, I would select Pittsburgh or New Orleans for the convention.

8. Compared with other cars, the BMW has highly sophisticated features.

9. Inquired Steve, "What major problems should the group consider first?"

10. Two ideas that came to me seemed brilliant.

11. The United States faces special problems in finance and in trade which will dominate the remainder of the century.

12. Harvard and Yale, whose reputations have remained at a high level over the years, provide graduates with special benefits.

13. Whoever serves this company well will receive two rewards.

14. The workers, still sullen and angry, made demands in pay and in benefits.

15. His early efforts failing, Clark tried other approaches.

16. The company has shown considerable neglect in the care of its grounds.

17. Before I considered any action, I sat down to make two plans.

18. Situated in Arizona, Tucson offers several advantages as the site of company headquarters.

19. To arrive at an agreement with the union, management made certain concessions.

20. Because of a superior staff and an influx of new capital, the company shows a bright future.

STAGE 3 WRAP-UP

☆ Do you feel the Power now? The three sentences of
1 2 2 form the basis for the total program. Write
several additional paragraphs if you need more
practice.

☆ In the Checklist below, check each item you have
mastered. Continue work on those items you have not
checked.

CHECKLIST

1. 1st Power sentence   ___

2. Two 2nd Power sentences   ___

3. Three clear sentences   ___

4. Three sentences in 10 minutes   ___

5. Grammar, spelling, punctuation   ___

6. Second opinion   ___

☆ Once satisfied with your seven paragraphs, move on to
Stage 4 for more Power.

The only prize much cared for by the powerful is power.
(Oliver Wendell Holmes, Jr.—1841 - 1935)

> *Go for the prize!*

STAGE 4

---

1 2 2 PARAGRAPHS
(10 minutes a day)

STAGE 4 INTRODUCES YOU TO. . .

☆ More writing of three-sentence paragraphs

☆ Creating your own 1st Power sentences

☆ 2nd Power links

☆ A summary of editing standards

FROM AN IDEA TO A 1st POWER SENTENCE

idea: concessions made by management

1st Power sentence: To arrive at an agreement with the union, management made two concessions.

idea: features of the BMW

1st Power sentence: Compared with other cars, the BMW has highly sophisticated features.

idea: two ways of relaxing after work

1st Power sentence: After work, I relax in two ways.

STAGE 4 ACTIVITY 1

☞ Turn the following ideas into 1st Power sentences.
See the Appendix for possible responses.

  1. two ways in which I enjoy my job

     (Start this sentence: "In two ways. . .")

  2. two motion pictures that portray some aspect of
     business life

     (Start this sentence: " Two motion
     pictures—names of shows—illustrate. . .")

  3. two favorite lunch spots

     (Start this sentence: " When I take a client to
     lunch, . . .")

  4. sessions Roger planned to attend at the convention

     (Start this sentence: "After reaching the
     convention center, Roger. . .")

  5. advantages offered by small businesses

     (Start this sentence: "Small businesses offer two
     advantages. . .")

  6. grating personalities in my office

     (Start this sentence: "On the way to my desk at
     the office, . . .")

7. two "games" that I see played on the job

(Start this sentence: "Every day. . .")

Create your own starters for these ideas.

8. health problems caused by stress

9. qualities of a good executive

10. construction problems caused by earthquakes

11. cars that I prefer for personal driving

12. outstanding leaders in my industry

Sentence possibilities for #8-#12

8. Stress causes two health problems.
   A person who suffers from stress may experience two
   health problems.

9. A good executive exhibits two special qualities.
   A good executive exhibits two qualities: leadership and
   character strength.

10. Earthquakes can cause two construction problems.
    Earthquakes may cause damage at construction sites.

11. For personal driving I prefer two cars.
    What two cars do I prefer for personal driving?

12. America has at least two dynamic corporate leaders.
    Business and industry have given the nation special
    leaders.

2nd POWER LINKS

☆ To make your writing clearer for your reader, use 2nd Power links to make the flow of thought easy to follow.

☆ These 2nd Power links make some connection to the 1st Power sentence.

☆ Certain words, such as those in the following chart, link a 2nd Power sentence to a 1st Power sentence. In addition to these specific links, you may repeat a word, words or idea from the 1st Power sentence.

2nd POWER LINKS

also	*first*	*one*
another	*furthermore*	*second*
besides	*moreover*	*to begin with*

Word, words or idea repeated from 1st Power

Examples:

Rain causes two problems at the construction site. One is floods. Another is mudslides.

Rain causes two problems at the construction site. Rain causes floods. Rain causes mudslides.

Rain causes floods and mudslides at the construction site. Floods prevent the pouring of concrete. Mudslides make a stable foundation difficult.

Rain causes two problems at the construction site. Rain angers workers. Rain worries management.

STAGE 4 ACTIVITY

☞ Using the 1st Power sentences that you created in Stage 4 Activity 1, write seven paragraphs of 1 2 2.

☞ Check each paragraph to make certain it has a 2nd Power link.

STAGE 4 MODELS

1. Eastman Kodak and Rockwell provide state-of-the-art programs to ease back pain. Because of a recent study revealing that back problems rank second to colds in causing employee absences, Kodak developed a back-care program. To relieve the pain associated with back problems, Rockwell has incorporated a wide range of fitness programs.

Back pain **makes the link in all three sentences.**

2. Memo

10/22/90

To: Liaison with City Council
From: Morgan Harris
Topic: Condition of local streets

The city of Los Angeles has shown considerable neglect in the care of the city streets in the area of company headquarters. The city rarely cleans the streets. The lampposts and street signs show need of repair.

Please discuss these concerns with the city council.

The links go from *neglect* **in the first sentence to** *rarely cleans* **in the second sentence to** *need of repair* **in the third sentence.**

How should a memo or letter of complaint end? With some suggestion of future action

3. Letter

9 January 1990

Dear Ms. Johnson:

I hope you will give us a chance to make up for the error of having misplaced your recent order. Please accept my personal apologies for the oversight. In addition, feel free to call me at any time about any problem you encounter.

Sincerely yours,

John Lee

This letter appears in block style, your choice or company policy.

The words *error* **and** *oversight* **make the links in the 1st and 2nd sentences.** *In addition* **makes the link in the 3rd sentence.**

4. Letter

22 Nov. 1990

Gentlemen:

On my recent trip to Europe on Alitalia, your service personnel deserved a real "pat on the back." At the ticket office in Rome, your people went out of their way to make certain I had my choice of seats and convenient times. I also want to compliment you on the fine treatment I received from the attendants on the airplane.

Sincerely,

Gary Remley

This letter appears in indented form. Letter form is subject to company, secretarial or personal preference.

Pat on the back links the first two sentences.

Also creates the link in the third sentence.

5.   Our newest product, Superfit, is the best package we have seen to start you on the road to fitness. All that your body needs with this package is one hour a day, three days a week. You can continue this Superfit program to whatever age you choose.

Product, package, program, and *Superfit* comprise the links.

6. In reply to your request for a recommendation for Marian Doubleday to act as a receptionist in your office, I can heartily praise her for two reasons. First, Mrs. Doubleday has a gracious manner in working with others. In addition to her pleasant attitude, she has an excellent telephone voice.

The linkage goes from *reasons* to *First* and *In addition*.

7. DR PEPPER retained an investment banking firm to explore investment alternatives. One possibility involved a merger with another company. A second possibility involved a sale of DR PEPPER assets to another company.

The word *alternatives* in the 1st Power sentence links with the words *One possibility* and *A second possibility*.

8. What qualities do you need to sell your product? Even if it means making a fool out of yourself, be persistent. Don't let the prospective buyer say, "I'll call you back after I think about it."

The 2nd and 3rd Power sentences describe *qualities*.

9. If you really want to get to the top of your company, you may have to join two clubs. Important clients love to be wined and dined at the club in the city, even if the food is mediocre. The country club, on the other hand, provides an ideal weekend retreat for yourself and other executives.

The word *clubs* ties the paragraph together.

10.   The modern corporate system offers something for everybody. The executives receive enormous salaries, stock options, and offices large enough in which their occupants can play jai alai. The secretarial, clerical, and reception personnel are offered medical plans, dental plans, pension plans, savings plans, continuing education plans, stop-smoking plans, lose-weight plans, and softball plans. Joe, the factory worker, gets regular five-minute breaks.

Link *everybody* **with all of the people listed.**

STAGE 4 ACTIVITY 3

☞ One can usually write three sentences in five minutes. Start a plan at this stage of daily writing of a 1 2 2 paragraph. Use any of the following suggestions, or write on any topic of your choice.

  1. clever billboard ads

  2. reasons for improving writing

  3. interesting people at the office

  4. ways that industry has changed

  5. qualities of a good manager

  6. problems facing the company for the remainder of the century

☞ Write one paragraph in memo format. Write another as a letter.

☞ Date your writings. Keep them in a file folder for future use.

☞ Include the word *two* in the 1st Power sentence, or use the concept of *two (see the 2nd Power link chart on page 21).*

STAGE 4 WRAP-UP

☆ Congratulations! You should feel good about the set of paragraphs you have written. Save them. You will use them in Stage 5.

☆ Have you been diligent about writing for 10 minutes a day?

☆ A neat handwritten, typed or printed piece of communication shows that you care about the reader. Frame the memo, letter or report on the page with appropriate margins (often one inch on all four sides of the paper).

CHECKLIST

1. Creating your own 1st Power sentence   ___

2. Two 2nd Power sentences   ___

3. Three complete sentences   ___

4. Three sentences in 10 minutes   ___

5. Grammar, spelling, punctuation   ___

6. Neatness and margins (important courtesy)   ___

7. Second opinion (someone you
   trust and respect)   ___

☆ Take a break. Cool off. Prepare yourself mentally for Stage 5, which will introduce you to five-sentence paragraphs.

Grant me the power of saying things.
(Coventry Patmore—1823-1896)

Give 3rd Power your best shot!

STAGE 5

1 2 3 2 3 PARAGRAPHS
(20 minutes 3 times a week)

STAGE 5 INTRODUCES YOU TO

☆ Five-sentence paragraphs

☆ 3rd Power sentences

☆ 3rd Power transitions

☆ Elimination of *there* at the beginning of sentences

3rd POWER SENTENCES

☆ Develop 2nd Power sentences

☆ Make writing more interesting through specific details

☆ Make some reference to 2nd Power sentences

☆ Use 3rd Power links through special words or through repetition of a word or idea

3rd POWER SIGNALS OR LINKS

consequently   *in other words*

for example   *specifically*

for instance   *to explain*

Word, words or idea repeated from 2nd Power

☆ Models for Word, words or idea repeated from 2nd Power

1. Rain causes two problems at the construction site. One is floods. Consequently, workers must delay the pouring of concrete. Another problem is mudslides. For example, it becomes difficult to put in a stable foundation.

    (1) Words like *consequently* **and** *for example* **link the 3rd Power sentences to the 2nd Power.**

2. Rain causes two problems at the construction site. Rain causes floods. Floods delay the pouring of concrete. Rain also causes mudslides. Mudslides interfere with creation of a stable foundation.

    (2) *Floods* **and** *mudslides* **form the links to the 2nd Power sentences.**

3. Rain causes floods and mudslides at the construction site. Floods prevent the pouring of concrete. That may result in worker layoffs. Mudslides make a stable foundation difficult. That, too, may result in labor delays, with possible layoffs.

(3) The word *That* forms the link between the 2nd and 3rd Power sentences.

4. Rain causes two problems at the construction site. Rain angers workers. They worry over possible job layoffs. Rain worries management. It frets about completing the building in time.

(4) The links go from *angers* to *worry* and from *worries* to *frets*.

ELIMINATION OF *THERE*

☆ Eliminating *there* from the beginning of a sentence will make your writing more precise.

☆ Think of *there* as a throwaway word. It does nothing for the meaning of a sentence.

☆ Your writing will have more power and effectiveness if you place meaningful words at the beginning of a sentence. Keep the action moving forward. Even though you hear and see the word "there" used every day, it does not make an effective opener.

☞ Look over the following examples of changing "there" openings:

1. There are two urgent problems facing the company.

   Two urgent problems are facing the company.

2. There are two business journals that vice-presidents should read.

Vice-presidents should read two business journals.

3. There are two cities the board should consider as convention sites.

The board should consider Pittsburgh and New Orleans as convention sites.

Activity for Elimination of *There*

☞   Rewrite the following sentences to eliminate *there*.

1. There are two special responsibilities that I have.

2. There are two kinds of vacations I enjoy.

3. There are two reasons to invest in AT&T.

4. There have been interesting on-the-job experiences in my career.

5. There are two special features about my product line.

☆ See the Appendix for some possible versions of the preceding five statements. Compare these with your own.

STAGE 5 MODELS

1. Improvement of your writing skills is important to both you and our company. First, excellent writing is part of the professional image we wish to present. Attention to detail in writing gives an overall impression that we will thoroughly attend to all of our clients' needs. Second, correspondence that effectively communicates your ideas can help you attain the goals for which you are writing. If your ideas demonstrate clear organization, good research, and brevity, your readers will have more confidence in your recommendations.

First and *Second* **link to** *you and our company.* *Image* **and** *impression* **link to each other.** *Ideas* **and** *ideas* **link to each other.**

2. You need to follow two basic strategies when you attend the seminar this weekend. To begin with, plan ahead by giving people at work your telephone number. If any major crisis occurs, they can reach you instantly. Second, make as many contacts as you possibly can. Networking is the key to expanding your client base by finding people with the same interests.

The links between the 2nd and 3rd Power sentences are in *telephone number* **and** *reach you* **and in** *contacts* **and** *Networking.*

3.   Our newest product, Superfit, is the best package we have seen to start you on the road to fitness. All that you will need for your body with this new package is one hour a day, three days a week. This will enable you to firm up all those flabby muscles that you thought would always look soft. You can continue the Superfit program to whatever age you choose. Dr. Leonard Goldman of the Olympic Training Center has stated that weight training is safe and effective for people of all ages.

Refer to this paragraph in Stage 4, page 24, to see how it went from three to five sentences.

4.   In reply to your request for a recommendation for Marian Doubleday to act as a receptionist in your office, I can heartily praise her for two reasons. First, Mrs. Doubleday has a gracious manner in working with others. She adeptly handles situations with our most difficult customers in the complaint department with tact and diplomacy. In addition to her pleasant attitude, she has an excellent telephone voice. Her well-modulated voice is firm yet flexible.

Re-read this paragraph in Stage 4, page 25. Observe how it became a Stage 5 here.

5.   Applicants can best impress a potential employer by emphasizing two important areas of qualification for the job. First, they must provide an outline of educational background. This should cover topics such as course title, a brief description of course content, degrees received, and schools attended. In addition, applicants need to summarize the experience they possess. This must be concisely written and carefully related to the prospective job.

The links go from *two areas* **to** *First* **to** *outline* **to** *This* **to** *In addition* **to** *summarize* **to** *This*.

6.   Rockwell, one of the world's great industrial leaders, has some helpful hints to prevent the fatigue corporate executives face. Always pace yourself to avoid burnout. If you can catch a half-hour nap in the middle of the day, you will feel more refreshed. It is also important to break up your schedule with a change of scenery. Just a short weekend trip can give you a whole new outlook on life.

This paragraph focuses on *helpful hints*. **The writer provides two such hints and explains each.**

7.   The modern corporation consists of two types of executives. At the very top is a chief executive. He spends his entire day posing for Annual Report photographs and testifying before Congress. Beneath the chief executive are several thousand executives engaged in "middle management." This is the corporate term for "management activities in which no one has any possible way to tell whether you're fouling up."

This paragraph illustrates humor in structured material. Structure does not ruin creativity.

8.   Hitachi's scientists and engineers have improved basic functions in engine control and information. They have created a multi-information system using a color thin filet transistor to display operating information, road maps, and a navigational system using these maps. With this system a driver could obtain a variety of driving information simply by touching the display screen. Hitachi has also developed a highly acclaimed hot-wire, air-flow sensor used in engine management. It helps achieve the diametrically opposed goals of maximum power and fuel economy.

This writer takes his second point to develop first. For variety, take the second point to develop first.

STAGE 5 WRITING ACTIVITIES

☞ On the average, you can write a five-sentence paragraph, memo or letter in 15 to 20 minutes. Take your file of 1 2 2 paragraphs from Stage 4 and expand them into 1 2 3 2 3 paragraphs of five sentences. They will have a 1st Power opener, two 2nd Power sentences, and two 3rd Power sentences.

☞ Write a five-sentence paragraph using any of these topics:

1. reasons for buying a product

2. interesting on-the-job experiences

3. special features of my company

4. tales that my secretary might relate

5. special responsibilities that I have

6. vacation places that I enjoy

☞ Maintain a writing schedule of 20 minutes a day, three days a week.

☞ Date your writings. Keep them in a file folder.

STAGE 5 WRAP-UP

☆ YOU PROBABLY WRITE BETTER NOW THAN
MOST OF THE PEOPLE YOU KNOW!

CHECKLIST

1. Structure of 1 2 3 2 3 paragraph   ___

2. 3rd Power sentences that
   relate clearly to 2nd Power   ___

3. Elimination of *there*   ___

4. Five sentences in 20 minutes   ___

5. Grammar, spelling, punctuation   ___

6. Neatness and margins (important courtesy)   ___

7. Second opinion (someone you
   trust and respect)   ___

☆ Does the Checklist show growth in your ability?
Good! Keep on *powering*.

☆ When you have written at least five paragraphs, have
edited them, and have shared them with someone,
move on to Stage 6. Be ready for a real challenge.

To be, or not to be, that is the question.
(Shakespeare—1564-1616)

> *To write well: that creates the answer.*

STAGE 6

---

1 2 3 2 3 PARAGRAPHS
(20 minutes, 3 times a week)

STAGE 6. . .

☆ Focuses on only one new item: the elimination of the verb *to be* from your writing.

THE VERB *TO BE*. . .

☆ Has eight forms:

> *is   am   are   was*
>
> *were   be   been   being*

☆ Results in weak statements. Use strong verbs.

1. Don is in a corporate law firm.
   Don handles corporate law cases.

2. I am a writer of proposals and resumés.
   I write proposals and resumés.

3. Helen and Sarah are typists.
   Helen and Sarah type.

4. Doug was at the office yesterday.
   Doug appeared at the office yesterday.

5. Betty and Ruth were away on Friday.
   Betty and Ruth spent Friday out of town.

6. Knowledge of computer operations can be useful.
   Knowledge of computer operations can prove useful.

7. Jim has been at the plant all day.
   Jim has worked at the plant all day.

8. Vern is being cautious in his decisions at board meetings.
   Vern makes decisions cautiously at board meetings.

ACTIVITY FOR *To Be*

☞ Rewrite the following sentences to eliminate forms of the verb *to be*:

   1. More accurate withholding is necessary under the new tax law.

   2. If I am eligible, I must file a return to receive a refund.

   3. Certain individuals are not eligible for the standard deduction.

4. This rule was effective for the 1985 tax year.

5. On the back of the form were two worksheets.

6. The income tax rate for individuals on net capital gains will not be more than 28%.

7. The old edition of the tax book has not been available since 1986.

8. Robert is being adamant in his stand against higher taxes.

☆ See Appendix, Stage 6, for some ways to eliminate *to be*.

STRONG ACTION VERBS

☆ Get a feel for verbs. They form the action and energy of a sentence.

☆ Study the following uses of strong verbs:

1. Dr. Ellis *directed* the company campaign against AIDS.

2. The secretary *took* responsibility for the errors in the letter.

3. Reed *organized* the staff into two teams.

4. The president *represented* the company at the convention.

5. Doug *conceived* the idea that changed the company's policy.

6. The executive *delegated* authority at the board meeting.

Activities for Strong Action Verbs

☞ Use the following action words in sentences. You may use the past tense. See the Appendix for some possibilities.

    1. manage

    2. give

    3. fuels

    4. increase

    5. hire

    6. expand

☞ Fold a sheet of paper in half the long way. On the left side of the page, list 10 nouns. Turn the paper over to the right column. Think of an occupation, like doctor, accountant, flight attendant. List 15 verbs on the right half of the page that go with that occupation. Try joining the nouns with the verbs to see what new combinations you can get. Finish the sentences, using verbs in the past tense if you need to.

STAGE 6 MODELS

1. IBM has always had two commitments. First, it has used high quality and high technology to design and build many kinds of products. Those products have gone into the home, the office, the hospital, and industry. A second commitment has gone beyond product—to a commitment to people. These have included marketing, service, and distribution people—all under strong and knowledgeable management.

The word *One* will almost force you to use *is*. Start a 2nd Power sentence with *First,*; then you will use strong verbs like *used, gone, included*.

2. Our company has put together a new product, Superfit, to start you on the road to fitness. Your body needs only one hour a day, three days a week, to become fit. That time will enable you to firm up all those flabby muscles that you thought would always look soft. You can continue the Superfit program to whatever age you choose. Dr. Leonard Goldman of the Olympic Training Center has stated that weight training has proven safe and effective for people of all ages.

Read this paragraph in Stage 5, page 34, to see how the *to be* verbs changed.

3.   Memo

24 Nov. 1990
To: Director of Research
From: CEO
Re: Dutch Touch Restaurants

For two reasons Van Doekker's
Dutch Touch Restaurants may
qualify as the next giant in
fast-food franchising. For one, the
product, sold as Panwiches,
capitalizes on local food prices,
adapts to regional and ethnic
tastes, and serves as snacks, main
course or dessert. For another, the
business offers operational
advantages. Food preparation
requires a small kitchen and
storage area, with no
sophisticated equipment.

You may wish to explore these
details further, for we may
consider investment in the
operation.

Strong verbs like
capitalize, adapts,
offers, requires **capture**
reader attention
more strongly than
the verb *to be.*

The writer adds the
final paragraph to
get action.

4.   In reply to your request for a
recommendation for Marian
Doubleday to act as a receptionist
in your office, I can heartily praise
her for two reasons. First, Mrs.
Doubleday has a gracious manner
in working with others. She has
repeatedly handled our most
difficult situations in the
complaint department with tact
and diplomacy. In addition to her
pleasant attitude, she has an
excellent telephone voice. Her
well-modulated voice
communicates firmness, yet
flexibility.

Read this paragraph
in Stage 5 to see how
the verbs *to be*
disappeared.

5. A card-access system will increase in-house security in two ways.

    First, only specific personnel may enter sensitive areas. This will restrict employees from wandering outside their work stations.

    Second, we can control the hours in which personnel can enter these areas. Ensuring the integrity of the company's classified rooms deserves top priority.

> This Stage 6 illustrates your freedom as a writer: to paragraph for possible effectiveness.

6. The modern corporation has two types of executives. At the very top you will find a chief executive. He spends his entire day posing for Annual Report photographs and testifying before Congress. Beneath the chief executive several thousand executives engage in *middle management*. In corporate language that means "management activities in which no one has any possible way to tell whether you've fouled up."

> This paragraph illustrates the use of humor.

7. Applicants can best impress a potential employer by emphasizing two important areas of qualification for the job. First, they must provide an outline of educational background. This should cover topics such as course titles, a brief description of course content, degrees received, and schools attended. In addition, applicants need to summarize their experience. The applicant must write this concisely, and he must relate it to the prospective job.

> Follow the line of strong verbs from the first to last sentences. Also, note the links between the various Powers.

8. In what ways might American businesses spend their generous contributions to economic education? For one, they might begin the development of such programs with a focus on specific objectives instead of stating a general objective like "promotion of free enterprise." Businesses must evaluate economic content for accuracy and objectivity. Second, businesses should not make *body counts* the sole criterion for the success of the program. Other measures of success include student attitude changes toward the study of economics and scores on economics achievement tests for the targeted grade levels.

> This paragraph has such strong verbs as *spend, begin, evaluate, make,* and *include.*
>
> As your writing becomes more advanced, the 2nd and 3rd Power links assume more importance. They make the material easier to read.

STAGE 6 ACTIVITIES

☞ From your file of paragraphs, rewrite all of your Stage 5s to eliminate all forms of the verb *to be.* You won't have to change your ideas, but you will enjoy the thinking process that will occur as you make changes.

☞ Every day, search in print—your daily newspaper or some magazine—to find a sentence using the verb *to be.* Take just a few moments to reword the sentence mentally to eliminate that verb.

STAGE 6 WRAP-UP

☆ At this stage, do you feel good about the ways you have been playing around with your basic ideas? Power Writing provides unexpected pleasures as you put pen to paper.

☆ If you want some ideas for writing, use any of the following:

1. aspects of my job that I enjoy

2. problems that I have on the job

3. interesting businesses in my town

4. two different uses of a company product

5. sounds that I hear on the job

6. what I would do with $10,000

CHECKLIST

1. Elimination of *there* —

2. Elimination of *to be* —

3. Structure of 1 2 3 2 3 paragraph —

4. Five sentences in 20 minutes —

5. Grammar, spelling, punctuation —

6. Neatness and margins (important courtesy) —

7. Second opinion (someone you trust and respect) —

☆ When you have written at least five paragraphs, have shared them with someone, and have met the Checklist requirements, go on to Stage 7.

☆ Do you feel comfortable with the time suggestion of 20 minutes a day for three days a week? Adjust that as you wish.

☆ Stage 7, which introduces the first set of Sentence Patterns, will help you develop a personal style. Go to it!

Next to the originator of a good sentence
is the first quoter of it.
(Emerson—1803-1882)

You're on the Road to Hemingway!

STAGE 7

---

1 2 3 2 3 PARAGRAPHS

WITH SENTENCE PATTERNING

(20 minutes, 3 times a week)

STAGE 7...

☆ Introduces you to Sentence Patterns

☆ Shows you how to mold, create, and sculpt sentences

☆ Directs you toward your own *unique* style

SENTENCE PATTERNS

☆ Congratulations on your use of Power to this point! You have control of 1st, 2nd, and 3rd Power. You have eliminated *there*. You use dynamic verbs. In a word, you have P-O-W-E-R!

☆ Now you start putting muscle into your writing. Push, pull, and jump in with pen in hand.

☆ The usual order of the English sentence goes from subject to verb to object. That order proves effective in much writing, but the English sentence has a wide variety of other structures. We will direct you to use of 14 of those patterns.

☆ Stage 7 presents the first four of the 14.

SENTENCE PATTERNS 1-2-3-4

1. Use strong action verbs.

2. Ask a question.

3. Open a sentence with an adverb.

4. Open a sentence with a prepositional phrase.

SENTENCE PATTERN # 1: USE STRONG ACTION VERBS

☆ This pattern focuses again on eliminating all forms of the verb *to be*, carried over from Stage 6.

☆ Study these models. Pay close attention to the strong verbs.

1. The problem *perplexed* the manager.

2. Amtrak *invested* millions of dollars in new equipment.

3. Economists *forecast* continued employment growth.

4. Mark *coordinated* policies among the various departments.

5. The chairman of the board *generated* much discussion with his opening remarks.

6. The foreman *implemented* the new policy with the workers in the plant.

Activity for Sentence Pattern # 1

☞　Use the following strong verbs to create sentences
without *there* and *to be*. See the Appendix for some
possible models.

　　1. rave

　　2. propose

　　3. receive

　　4. fire

　　5. ask

　　6. revolutionize

**SENTENCE PATTERN # 2:
ASK A QUESTION**

☆ Instead of facts, use questions to start sentences. This
way you state your main point with the question. The
rest of the writing develops the answer.

☆ Begin your questions with one of these words: *who,
what, when, where, why,* or *how.*

☆ **Models**

1. Who sets company policies?

2. What steps occur on the assembly line?

3. When do the rules go into effect?

4. Where might one find good working conditions?

5. Why do microwave ovens look like television sets?

6. How does Japanese industry differ from American industry?

Activity for Sentence Pattern # 2

☞   Write questions avoiding the verb *to be*. See the Appendix for possibilities.

    1. who

    2. what

    3. when

    4. where

    5. why

    6. how

SENTENCE PATTERN # 3:
START A SENTENCE WITH AN ADVERB

☆ Emphasize *how, when, where, why, how much, how many times* at the beginning of a sentence.

☆ **Models**

1. Carefully, the board considered Icahn's offer. (How?)

2. Tomorrow, company headquarters will move to Pittsburgh. (When?)

3. Locally, our company products sell well. (Where?)

4. Because the president had died, Sullivan Inc. closed its plant. (Why?)

5. Seldom does the manager call a staff meeting. (How often?)

6. Frequently, the treasurer leaped to his feet in protest. (How many times?)

Activity for Sentence Pattern # 3

☞ Write sentences that start with the following adverbs and that eliminate the verb *to be*. See the Appendix for samples.

    1. soon (when)

    2. sharply (how)

    3. today (when)

4. desperately (how)

5. temporarily (how many times)

6. recently (when)

SENTENCE PATTERN # 4:
START A SENTENCE WITH A PREPOSITIONAL PHRASE

☆ Picture the construction of a building in your area.
Vertical shafts zoom straight upward from the earth.
Crossbeams act as bridges connecting one shaft with
another. Prepositions act like those crossbeams. They
connect different parts of a sentence with each other.

☆ Punctuation: Use a comma after a natural pause.
Check yourself by re-reading your sentence for flow.

☆ **Models** (with the prepositional phrases in italics)

1. *During the day,* Booth spent four hours on the road.

2. *Despite the much-chronicled decline* of heavy industry in
America, the blue-collar labor market still has pockets of
strength.

3. *In California,* even more than in most political realms,
style often counts more than substance.

4. *Of newly appointed chief executive officers* in 1985, 44%
came from either technical or operational backgrounds.

5. *Without plan or purpose,* the chairman conducted an
informal meeting.

6. *At that precise moment,* the telephone rang.

Activity for Sentence Pattern # 4

☞ Write sentences that start with the following prepositions. Avoid the verb *to be*. See the Appendix for samples.

1. despite

2. through

3. in

4. within

5. in spite of

6. without

STAGE 7 MODELS

Sentence Pattern numbers 1-2-3-4 appear in the right margin.

1. Our company has put together a new product, Superfit, to start you on the road to fitness. In just one hour a day for three days a week, this program will get you into shape. This regimen will enable you to firm up all those flabby muscles that you thought would always look soft. You can continue the Superfit program to whatever age you choose. Dr. Leonard Goldman of the Olympic Training Center has stated, "Weight training has proven safe and effective for people of all ages. It can extend your life and improve its quality."

> 4
> **The prepositional phrase opener emphasizes the time to get you into shape.**

2. Recently, we took over ownership of a camping equipment store, but we have not reached a decision on which portable tents we will purchase. We need some explanatory information on the construction of your new nylon tents. This will help us to decide whether these or the canvas tents can provide what we need. Also, what information do you have on the durability of your product? Specifically, how many years of service will an ordinary tent provide?

> 3
> **The adverb opener gives attention to the time.**
>
> **The questions request answers.**
>
> 2

3. In reply to your request for a recommendation for Marian Doubleday to act as a receptionist in your office, I can heartily praise her for two reasons. First, Mrs. Doubleday has a gracious manner in working with others. Repeatedly she has handled our most difficult situations in the complaint department with tact and diplomacy. In addition to her pleasant attitude, she possesses an excellent telephone voice. With firmness and flexibility, her well-modulated voice communicates a warm strength.

4
The prepositional phrase opener gives attention to the person making the request.

3
The adverb emphasizes frequency.

1
4
Even though *In addition to* is a prepositional phrase, it is first a transition or link and cannot be labeled a (4).

4. In preparing a powerful memo, use the two key components of clarity and conciseness. To make your points convincing, use the active rather than the passive verb. This will enable you to say exactly what you mean. Second, eliminate all unnecessary words or sentences that do not directly relate to your main idea. Malcolm Baldridge, former Commerce Secretary, stated, "Vigorous writing requires not that the writer should make all sentences short, but that every word count."

4
Emphasizes when

5. By contrast with the Los Angeles area, Humboldt County will allow your $50,000 to go considerably further. A three-bedroom home on a half-acre in Humboldt costs 60% less than a comparable residence in West Los Angeles. Unlike its crowded neighbor to the south, Humboldt makes it possible for young families to qualify immediately for a start on investing in a home. In addition, when it comes to eating out in Humboldt, people find it difficult to spend more than $50 for two in any of the county's better restaurants. What a pleasure to dine out three times a week and spend the same as one meal at Trump's, a trendy West Hollywood spot!

    4
    The prepositional phrase opener prepares the reader for Humboldt County.
    1
    4
    The prepositional phrase opener sets up contrast.

    Some links are adverbs and prepositional phrases in structure, but they do not count as sentence openers. The sentence officially opens after the link.

6. Once again, *Newsweek* has scored a first in the coverage of important regional issues that other national magazines have failed to notice. I refer specifically to the success in higher test scores in the Alabama public schools. You pointed out quite correctly that test scores in reading and writing improved more than 12% over last year. In addition, an article concerning the business and industrial development around Mobile has generated much interest. Already, two top industrial firms have decided on new plant locations in our area.
    We can use this information in recruiting new employees.

    3
    The adverb opener emphasizes the time element.

    3
    The adverb opener again calls attention to time.

STAGE 7 ACTIVITIES

☞   From your file of paragraphs, rewrite your Stage 6s to include the first four Sentence Patterns. Put at least one of the Sentence Patterns into each paragraph. In one paragraph, you might experiment with using more than one pattern, but do not feel that you must always vary every sentence. Do not consider the links as sentence openers. The sentence officially opens *after* the link.

☆ In publications you encounter in your daily life and work, search for these first four patterns.

Examples:

1. Trump has operated close to a decade in turning expectations and promotion into hard profits. (strong verb pattern) (*Los Angeles Times*, 2/28/88)

2. How do you turn small business into smart business? (question pattern) (*Business Week*, 2/22/88)

3. Nonetheless, few would deny that the Japanese have made great strides as inventors. (adverb opener pattern) (*Time*, 3/21/88)

4. With uncertainty stalking the markets, every portfolio needs a safety corner. (prepositional phrase opener) (*Financial World*, 2/9/88)

☞   Start a Sentence Pattern Journal. Here's how. Record a pattern a day copied from print. Add your own original sentence using the new pattern.

Example: Pattern # 4: Open a sentence with a prepositional phrase.

At conferences where people start talking about issues first, the proceedings become stiff and sides can get polarized. (*Harvard Business Review*, May-June 1987)

After several weeks of writing, I can see improvement. (original sentence)

STAGE 7 WRAP-UP

☆ Even though your writing may not compare with Hemingway's, you must know that your writing has changed considerably since Stage 1. Do you feel good about that?

☆ How does your schedule fit in with the suggested time plan of 20 minutes a day for three days a week? Adjust that as you need to.

☆ Use the following ideas for more writing. Aim at a new 1 2 3 2 3 paragraph for those 20 minutes. In each new paragraph, work in at least one of the first four Sentence Patterns.

1. ways to prevent hotel thefts

2. ways to conserve energy in the home

3. kinds of television ads

4. methods of addressing an audience

5. ways in which you consider time as money

6. ways in which company officers abuse expense accounts

CHECKLIST

1. Use of Sentence Patterns 1-2-3-4   ___

2. Elimination of *there*   ___

3. Elimination of *to be*   ___

4. Structure of 1 2 3 2 3 paragraph   ___

5. Five sentences in 20 minutes   ___

6. Grammar, spelling, punctuation   ___

7. Neatness and margins (important courtesy) ___

8. Second opinion (someone you trust and respect) ___

☆ After you have written at least five paragraphs that meet the Checklist standards and have received approval from your personal editor, move to Stage 8.

☆ Just as each brick in your headquarters building fits into place to form the whole structure, so Power sentences fit into a paragraph to communicate a clear thought. Stage 8 will add two new sentences to your Stage 7 to present three points about your idea. Go to it!

What I tell you three times is true.
(Lewis Carroll—1832-1898)

> *A Stage 8, like Gaul, divides into three parts.*

STAGE 8

1 2 3 2 3 2 3 PARAGRAPHS

(30 minutes, twice a week)

STAGE 8. . .

☆ Expands the five-sentence paragraph into a seven-sentence paragraph

☆ Introduces three new Sentence Patterns

1 2 3 2 3 2 3 PARAGRAPHS

☆ To create the seven-sentence paragraph, take any Stage 7 paragraph and add one more 2nd Power and one more 3rd Power sentence.

☆ Good speakers command your immediate respect. They give you a road map to follow. They preorder and number their main points. You remember what they say. Apply this technique to your writing.

☆ In the 1st Power sentence of your Stage 7 paragraph, change *two* to *three*. You will now write about. . .

+ three reasons

+ three causes

+ three purposes

☆ Use of *three* will keep you on target to develop your major and minor details.

MODEL STAGE 8 CREATED FROM A STAGE 7

For three reasons Van Doekker's Dutch Touch Restaurants may qualify as the next giant in fast-food franchising. First, the product, sold as Panwiches, capitalizes on local food prices, adapts to regional and ethnic tastes, and serves as snacks, main course or dessert. These advantages give the product a wide market. Second, the business offers operational benefits. Food preparation requires a small kitchen and storage area, with no sophisticated equipment. Third, the franchiser, CutCo, has a history of franchise successes. CutCo assists licensees in virtually every aspect of opening and operating.

Three **in the 1st Power sentence makes it possible for the reader to move rapidly with the help of links** *First, Second,* **and** *Third.* **The 3rd Power sentences clearly link to the 2nd Power sentences.**

STAGE 8 ACTIVITY 1

☞ Take any three of the Stage 7s you have written. In the 1st Power sentence, just change *two* to *three*. Add a 2nd Power and 3rd Power sentence on the end of each paragraph. *Voilà*! A Stage 8!

SENTENCE PATTERNS 5-6-7

5. Use an appositive.

6. Open a sentence with an adverbial clause.

7. Use parallel structure in words, phrases, clauses, and sentences.

SENTENCE PATTERN # 5:
USE AN APPOSITIVE

☆ Note the following appositives:

Mary, the office manager,

Sacramento, California's capital,

The subject equals the appositive.

- ☆ *Opposite* refers to *away from; apposite* refers to *near.*

- ☆ Appositives—nouns or pronouns—extend the meaning of preceding nouns or pronouns. They re-state and define a nearby word.

- ☆ **Models**

1. The Santa Barbara Biltmore, a jewel in the crown of Central Coast hotels, received a fresh sheen from its new owners, the Four Seasons.

   (*A jewel in the crown* re-states or explains the *Biltmore.*)

2. I refer to Ford the auto-maker, not Ford the President.

   (When the appositives have a close relationship with the nouns they re-state or define, the comma has tended to disappear.)

3. The company plane landed at Port-au-Prince, the capital of Haiti.

   (Port-au-Prince is the capital; the capital is Port-au-Prince.)

4. Throughout the industry, retail-management graduates typically start out in the $18,000 to $24,000 range, salaries that might double or triple in several years as the graduates scale the managerial ranks.

   (*Range* and *salaries* are nouns in apposition.)

5. Internship programs, usually cooperative efforts between a company and a high school or university, integrate classroom studies with planned and supervised work experience.

   (*Programs* and *efforts* are the nouns in apposition.)

6. Dick Anderson, a one-time reporter and dogged historical researcher, provided some thoughtful data at the meeting.

   (*A one-time reporter* and *researcher* defines *Anderson*.)

Activity for Sentence Pattern # 5

☞ Create sentences with the following nouns in apposition: (See the Appendix for possible models.)

   1. Lee Iacocca, the Chrysler chairman of the board,

   2. General Motors, the largest American car manufacturer,

3. Sanyo, a firm that

4. The board decided to hold its March meeting in Atlanta, site of

5. Donald Trump, the astounding New York entrepreneur,

6. Japan, one of our closest allies,

**SENTENCE PATTERN # 6:
START A SENTENCE WITH AN
ADVERBIAL CLAUSE**

☆ The following words open adverbial clauses:

after	*as if*	*since*	*when*
although	*because*	*though*	*whenever*
as	*before*	*until*	*while*

☆ When adverbial clauses open a sentence, they should be followed by a comma.

☆ **Models**

1. Since communication satellites began circling the Earth as the relay towers of the Global Village, the world has become a smaller place.

2. After Alderson assumed control of the company, it flourished.

3. As the hours passed, Vern's energy level mounted.

4. Unless unexpected delays occur, the workers will finish the new wing by spring.

5. While the manager and I walked around the plant, he explained various operations to me.

6. Before I could even rise to my feet to defend myself, the chairman ended the session.

Activity for Sentence Pattern # 6

☞ Create sentences that start with the following words. Add the comma at the pause you hear when you read the sentence aloud. See the Appendix for some models.

1. because

2. although

3. whenever

4. until

5. though

6. when

SENTENCE PATTERN # 7:
USE PARALLEL STRUCTURE IN WORDS, PHRASES, AND SENTENCES

☆ Think of railroad tracks, which run parallel to each other. If one track bends along the line, a train goes off the rails. The same thing happens to a reader. He goes off the track of logical thought if ideas don't run parallel.

☆ **Models**

1. Southern California's decades-long business boom, its growing status as a Pacific Rim financial center, and its affluent population have made Southern California fertile soil over the years for lawyers and accountants, doctors and dentists.

   (The parallelism lies in the three words: *boom, status, population.*)

2. One-time Harvard professor Thornton T. Bradshaw consults for General Electric, chairs the MacArthur Foundation, sits on five corporate boards, and heads several journalistic and education organizations.

   (The verbs keep the thought parallel: *consults, chairs, sits, heads.*)

3. Jobs in the Los Angeles Unified School District run the gamut from teachers to custodians, psychologists to cafeteria workers, bus drivers to police.

   (The parallelism lies in the listing of the jobs.)

4. The biggest retail stores employ a diverse work force that includes salespeople, managers, buyers, finance experts, and those in marketing and promotion.

   (The parallelism lies in the listing of those in the work force.)

5. The country grocery store stocks canned goods, fresh meat, bread and crackers, flour, fencing, nails, hammers, and guns.

(The parallelism lies in the series of nouns.)

Activity for Sentence Pattern # 7

☞ Write sentences using the following parallel sets. See the Appendix for models.

1. Los Angeles, New York, and London

2. General Motors, Ford Motor Company, and Chrysler Motors

3. Lee Iacocca, Donald Trump, and Carl Icahn

4. to the farm, to the factory, and to the home

5. Wherever I have gone, wherever I go, and wherever I will go,

6. with regret, with appreciation, and with hope (You might use this opening as part of a letter of resignation.)

STAGE 8 MODELS

Sentence Pattern numbers 5-6-7 appear in the right margin.

1.   Our company has put together a special product, Superfit, to start you on the road to fitness. In just one hour a day for three days a week, this program will get you into shape. This regimen will enable you to firm up all those flabby muscles that you thought would always look soft. If you start this weight-training program now, you can continue exercising to whatever age you want. Dr. Leonard Goldman of the Olympic Training Center says, "Weight training has proven safe and effective for people of all ages." We can offer you the Superfit Package, which includes two sets of dumbbells and a total exercise program, for the low price of $34.50. One month at your average health club would cost more than this total package.

5
Re-read this paragraph in Stage 7, page 56, to see how this version added a third point and explained it.

6

2. In reply to your request for a recommendation for Marian Doubleday to act as a receptionist in your office, I can heartily praise her gracious manner, her well-modulated voice, and her typing ability. Because of her gracious manner, she works well with all types of people. She has repeatedly handled, with tact and diplomacy, our most difficult situations in the complaint department. In addition to her pleasant attitude, she possesses an excellent telephone voice. Firm but flexible, her voice radiates a warm strength. Furthermore, Mrs. Doubleday, a former reporter, has developed into a competent typist. Her typing speed exceeds sixty words per minute, with no errors.

3. As an irate Volvo owner, I feel it necessary to write this letter of complaint. For one thing, the car has proven unreliable. As I drove it around town on several occasions, it stalled and required towing to a garage. For another, the car has proven too costly to own. The towing charges and frequent repair bills have cost me several hundred dollars. Above all, even after I gave your service department a firm reminder, it failed to check the alternator carefully. The time invested to return the car has resulted in my losing two full days of production time.

    I would appreciate some response to this letter.

How to write without the *three*:

7
In this paragraph the writer puts the three qualities of Marian Doubleday in the first sentence. Then he develops them one at a time.

5

6
This possible letter has a final paragraph requesting action.

6
You probably won't get a new Volvo, but you certainly should hear from the company.

4.   If a company considers car leasing, it might look to the three advantages offered by Hertz. First, Hertz gives a choice of any car make and model to meet fleet needs. These include both domestic and foreign cars. Second, Hertz has done something about maintenance costs. A team of automotive experts deals directly with any repair shop via a special toll-free number. Third, Hertz will assign to a company a local personal account executive. He makes sure that the fleet operates at top efficiency.

6
All but the first sentence of this paragraph follow the subject-verb structure. The use of the adverbial clause in the first sentence adds a touch of style.

5.   The modern corporation has four levels of personnel: the chief executive, "middle management," tens of thousands of workers, and "Bud." At the top you will find a chief executive. He spends his day posing for Annual Report photographs and testifying before several thousand executives engaged in "middle management." This corporate term covers "management activities in which no one can possibly tell that you've fouled up." Beneath that second group you will find tens of thousands of secretarial, clerical, and reception personnel. Beneath that group, somewhere in a factory nobody ever goes to because it has no decent place around it where you can have lunch, you have the actual production work force. This consists of a grizzled old veteran employee named "Bud."

Why four, not three?

This paragraph shows a variation in Power.

7
It lets you know that you don't have to restrict yourself to *two* or *three* points. . . that you can do with ideas what you wish to communicate.

7
Also note that the third group does not have a 3rd Power sentence to explain it. Again, Power gives you that kind of freedom.

6.   When companies operate on an international basis, they often encounter three major obstacles. To begin with, economic problems present real uncertainty in most countries. Creeping inflation occurs worldwide, regardless of the level of prosperity. In addition, some countries have grown increasingly nationalistic against multi-national companies. To avoid this situation, firms must hire first-rate marketing organizations to improve their image. Last, establishing firm management control will eliminate the inconsistency of many company policies. Nothing ensures a company's credibility better than presenting a unified, straightforward approach.

6
What occurs here?

In seven sentences this paragraph has three different sentence openers (*To avoid*, an infinitive opener, and *establishing*, a gerund opener). Three patterns in seven sentences make for good styling.

7. In what three ways might American businesses spend their generous contributions to economic education? For one, they might begin with a focus on specific objectives, instead of stating a general objective like "promotion of free enterprise." Businesses must evaluate all economic content for accuracy and objectivity. Second, businesses should not make "body counts" the sole criterion for the success of the program. Other measures of success include student attitude changes toward the study of economics and scores on economic achievement tests for the targeted grade levels. Third, businesses must recognize the problem of the teachers' own lack of economic knowledge. If they identified interested teachers, businesses could provide them with special seminars.

Refer to Stage 6 to see how this paragraph changed from five to seven sentences.

It also re-worded the final sentence to use a Stage 8 Sentence Pattern.

6

STAGE 8 ACTIVITY 2

☆ Don't let writing seven sentences intimidate you. You have what it takes to go on.

☆ Even though a completed Stage 8 looks overwhelming, remember that you added only two sentences to a Stage 7 to create a Stage 8.

☞ From your file of 1 2 3 2 3 paragraphs, select any three to develop into Stage 8s. Change *two* in the 1st Power sentence to *three* and add the new 2nd and 3rd Power sentences to create a seven-sentence paragraph.

☞   You can do this daily practice in a few moments because you create only two new sentences, retaining the original five. Use the new Sentence Patterns 5-6-7 in the two new sentences you create.

☞   Look for the three new sentence patterns in your daily reading.

☞   Continue your daily Sentence Pattern journal, with one copied model and one original sentence.

STAGE 8 WRAP-UP

☆ Do you feel comfortable with the suggested time schedule for Stage 8—30 minutes twice a week? Keep adjusting your time for writing to fit your daily schedule.

☆ It will take you 20 to 30 minutes to create a new seven-sentence paragraph.

☆ If you need ideas for writing, try the following:

1. three words to describe the personality of one of your executives (You may not wish to show this paragraph to him/her!)

2. types of suppliers your business depends on

3. sections of a department store which could use remodeling

4. ways that a charitable organization spends money

5. steps that the company can take to prevent routine from becoming depressing for employees

6. effects that trucking has upon the economy

☆ Stage 8 makes it possible for you to write a memo, letter or report of any length. You can now write about four reasons, five ways, six purposes—any number of things.

☆ By now you should have no difficulty in adding 4th Power, 5th Power, 6th Power, any Power sentences to develop your main idea.

☆ It's time to Power lunch with your editing colleague. Of course, it's on you!

CHECKLIST

1. Structure of 1 2 3 2 3 2 3 paragraph   ____

2. Use of Sentence Patterns 5-6-7   ____

3. Elimination of *there*   ____

4. Elimination of *to be*   ____

5. Seven sentences in 30 minutes   ____

6. Grammar, spelling, punctuation   ____

7. Neatness and margins (important courtesy)   ____

8. Second opinion   ____

☆ After you have written at least three Stage 8 paragraphs that meet your Checklist standards, move to Stage 9. Keep going!

Variety's the very spice of life.
(Cowper—1731-1800)

Spice it up!

STAGE 9

VARIATIONS IN PLACEMENT OF 1ST POWER SENTENCES
(30 minutes, twice a week)

STAGE 9. . .

☆ Builds upon the Stage 8 paragraphs by changing the order of the 1st Power sentence in each paragraph

☆ Introduces four new sentence patterns

VARIATION A: 1ST POWER AS THE LAST SENTENCE

☆ Through Stages 4-5-6-7-8, you have placed your main idea at the beginning of a paragraph. Then you have developed that idea with appropriate details. You will now learn to use other structures by varying the placement of the main idea. Variation A presents a group of details, then summarizes them in the last sentence as a conclusion or summary. Polishing touches (signals) often introduce that conclusion.

POLISHING TOUCHES

as a result	*I conclude that*	*to sum up*
as one can see	*in conclusion*	*in summary*
for these reasons	*in short*	*to conclude*

Model for Variation A

Because of her gracious manner, Marian Doubleday works well with all types of people. With tact and diplomacy, she has repeatedly handled our most difficult situations in the complaint department. In addition, to hear her voice on the telephone provides a soothing feeling. Firm but flexible, her well-modulated voice radiates a warm strength. Furthermore, Mrs Doubleday, a former reporter, has developed into a competent typist. Her typing speed exceeds sixty words per minute, with no errors. In summary, these strong qualities rate Mrs. Doubleday top consideration for the available position.

These strong qualities **in the final sentence provide the summary for the paragraph.**

8
To hear **is an infinitive sentence opener. Remember that the link,** *In addition to*, **does not officially open the sentence.**

Activity for Variation A

☞ Select one of your Stage 8 paragraphs. Reword it to move the 1st Power sentence to last position. Try to use one of the polishing touches. Also, try to use Sentence Pattern # 8, explained later in this Stage 9 section.

VARIATION B: 1ST POWER AS FIRST AND LAST SENTENCES

Put your main idea as both the first and last sentences of a paragraph. This works well for longer material. First, inform the reader of your main idea. Then summarize it at the end of the paragraph to make certain the reader has stayed on target.

Model for Variation B

Our newest product, Superfit, will start you on the road to fitness. For one thing, the program requires only one hour a day, three days a week. Superfit will enable you to firm up all those flabby muscles that you thought would always look soft. Starting this weight training now, you can continue exercising to whatever age you want. Dr. Leonard Goldman of the Olympic Training Center has stated, "Weight training has proven safe and effective for people of all ages." We can offer you the Superfit package, which includes two sets of dumbbells and a total exercise program, for the low price of $34.50. One month at your average health club would cost more than this total package. As you can see—because of its cost-competitiveness and immediate results—buy Superfit NOW!

When you put the main idea into both the first and last sentences, make sure the wording is not identical

9
This sentence starts with the present participle *starting*.

Activity for Variation B

☞ Select one of your Stage 8 paragraphs. Reword it to put the 1st Power sentence in first and last positions. Try to use one of the Polishing Touches. Also, try to use Sentence Pattern #9, explained later in this Stage 9 section.

VARIATION C: 1ST POWER ANYWHERE

Actually, you may place your main idea anywhere in a paragraph, as long as you make the sequence of supporting details clear to the reader.

Model for Variation C

One improvement at Century Park East—insulation—will provide for the well-being of the occupants by resisting conduction of heat and cold. If a building does not have insulation, much of the heat passes through the walls and ceiling. Added to the process of insulation, two other improvements will save on fuel bills and increase the comfort of the residents in the building. Weatherstripping around the windows and doors will safeguard against air infiltration. To make sure that the weatherstripping remains watertight, we should seal the windows and install window latches. Caulking, another improvement, provides an airtight seal between the windows and building materials. Immediately after weatherstripping, we should begin the caulking process.

This paragraph has two sentences before the main idea. They discuss one of the improvements before the writer tells you he plans to write about two others.
10
Pattern #10 opens a sentence with a past participle (*Added*).

8
Pattern #8 opens a sentence with an infinitive.

Activity for Variation C

☞ Select one of your Stage 8 paragraphs. Reword it to put the 1st Power sentence in any other position than first or last. Try to use Sentence Pattern #10, explained in this Stage 9 section.

VARIATION D: 1ST POWER IMPLIED

☆ Sometimes you may not want to include a 1st Power sentence at all. Imply or infer it from the sentences of detail. Just be sure you express your details clearly so that the reader can follow the main idea easily.

Model for Variation D

As a corporate woman, I have found that unwanted advances have become a normal part of my life. Learning to cope with the insistent men who don't take "no" for an answer keeps me on guard, and sitting in conference meetings with such men makes it difficult to maintain a professional attitude. More than I care to relate, lost luggage poses another problem. Last month, for instance, two of my bags went to another destination, forcing me to spend more than $100 on basics in a hotel shop. On top of those two annoyances, I find that spending so much time at airport hotels always raises my anxiety level. When I finally do arrive home, my husband often bears the brunt of my complaints.

In a paragraph of implication, make sure that your details lead the reader to your point.

11
In this paragraph, *unwanted advances, lost luggage,* and *spending time at airport hotel*s all add up to annoyances for a corporate woman.

Pattern #11 is a compound sentence.

Activity for Variation D

☞ Select one of your Stage 8 paragraphs. Reword it to imply the 1st Power thought. Try to use Sentence Pattern #11, explained later in this Stage 9 section.

VARIATION E: 1ST POWER SIGNALED BY RED-ALERT WORDS

☆ Picture a space rocket, moving on course. Ground control wants to signal the crew to change direction. A red light begins to flash in the cabin of the spaceship.

☆ Something close to that can happen in a paragraph. Alert your reader when you want to change direction in your thinking. Use one of the Red-Alert Signals.

RED-ALERT SIGNALS
but
however
nevertheless
on the contrary
otherwise
regardless

☆ These Red-Alert Signals inform the reader that what has preceded served as introduction, background or contrast. Now the writer intends to present and develop his main idea.

☆ Such sentences preceding the Red-Alert Signal have Zero (0) Power. Without them and without the Red-Alert Signal, the paragraph will make sense.

Model for Variation E

Operating just within their own national boundaries, many companies encounter problems. But, once they move to the international level, they may face three major obstacles. To begin with, economic difficulties present real uncertainty in most countries. Creeping inflation occurs worldwide, regardless of the level of prosperity. In addition, some countries have grown increasingly nationalistic against multi-national firms. To avoid this situation, companies must hire first-rate marketing organizations to improve their image. Last, establishing firm management control will eliminate the inconsistency of many company policies. Nothing ensures a company's credibility better than presenting a unified, straightforward approach.

9
Galbraith imitation: John Kenneth Galbraith uses this variation often in his writings on the industrial state. This paragraph has one Zero (0) sentence before Red-Alert *But,* which introduces the main idea. Pattern #9 is a present participial sentence opener.
8
Pattern #8 is an infinitive opener.

Activity for Variation E

☞ Select one of your Stage 8 paragraphs. Reword it to use a Red-Alert Signal. Try to use one of the four new Sentence Patterns: #8-#9-#10-#11.

SUMMARY OF VARIATIONS

```
LOCATIONS OF 1ST POWER SENTENCES

                First
                 Last
            First and Last
              Anywhere
               Implied
         Signaled by Red-Alerts
```

☆ You now have written all of the basic structures of paragraphs. You have accomplished much in a short time. Perseverance has paid off!

SENTENCE PATTERNS 8-9-10-11

8. Open a sentence with an infinitive.

   (the "to" form of the verb: *to work*)

9. Open a sentence with a present participle.

   (the "ing" form of the verb: *working*)

10. Open a sentence with a past participle.

   (often the "ed" form of the verb: *worked*)

11. Use a compound sentence.

☆ The Stage 9 variations earlier in this section labeled the four new Sentence Patterns in the right margin. Writing activities directed you to use each of them in your own variations. Now you have the explanations, models, and exercises for them.

SENTENCE PATTERN #8:
OPEN A SENTENCE WITH AN INFINITIVE

☆ The infinitive is the "to" form of the verb:
to write, to read, to speak, to listen.

☆ Use a comma if you hear a pause when you read a sentence aloud. Also use a comma to emphasize the opening of a sentence.

☆ **Models**

1. To prosper, Odetics must find practical uses for its robotic technology.

2. To compete, our company must boost product quality.

3. To resolve issues, each of us has to take a good look at the other's point of view.

4. To handle information, our company has created the Chief Information Officer (CIO) position.

5. To cope with the new tax law, our accountants should attend the seminar in Sacramento.

6. To enter the San Francisco market, our company needs to place an agent there.

Activity for Sentence Pattern # 8

☞ Complete the following infinitive openers. See the Appendix for samples.

1. to understand

2. to do the job better and faster,

3. to finance

4. to attend the committee meeting,

5. to have fluency in Spanish,

6. to negotiate,

SENTENCE PATTERN # 9:
OPEN A SENTENCE WITH A PRESENT PARTICIPLE

☆ The "ing" part of a verb forms the present participle:
go = going; write = writing. It functions as an adjective.

☆ **Models**

1. Conducting his people-to-people program at a private level, President Carter breakfasted with John Shanklin, 71, an employee of Washington's Sheraton-Carlton Hotel.

2. Writing rapidly, Phil finished the report before the meeting.

3. Raising his hand, Mike silenced the irate members of the board.

4. Stepping up to the door, Tom saw that the other members of the board had already assembled.

5. Waiting at the airport, Steve reviewed what had gone wrong on his sales call.

6. Pounding the gavel, Donald called the session to order.

Activity for Sentence Pattern # 9

☞ Complete the following present participial sentence openers. See the Appendix for samples.

1. Failing to remain solvent,

2. Reacting to sanctions against South Africa,

3. Signing the contract for the computer lease,

4. Sitting alone in Sheraton's executive conference room,

5. Judging the current economic indicators,

6. Finding the information he needed about company health insurance,

SENTENCE PATTERN # 10:
OPEN A SENTENCE WITH A PAST PARTICIPLE

☆ The past participle = the third principal part of the verb (satisfied, compared, overtaken). It usually ends in "ed." It is an adjective.

☆ When a past participial phrase opens a sentence, use a comma following it.

☆ **Models**

1. Impressed by the ceremony and deeply moved by the speeches, the sales force left the auditorium in silence.

2. Compared with the thousands of U.S., Soviet, and West European supersonic airplanes that crisscross the skies, the tiny Concorde fleet could not possibly have much impact on the ozone.

3. Exhausted physically, the computer operator rested after a long day's work.

4. Annoyed at the paperwork on his desk, Roger decided to take the afternoon off.

5. Satisfied that the meeting had gone well, Peter drove home with positive thoughts.

6. Moved to a larger location, the headquarters staff operated much more smoothly.

Activity for Sentence Pattern #10

☞ Complete the following past participial phrase sentence openers. See the Appendix for samples.

1. Driven with ambition,

2. Renovated four years ago,

3. Persuaded by the chairman,

4. Based on recent sales,

5. Bypassed in office promotions,

6. Promised the next vice-presidency,

SENTENCE PATTERN #11: USE A COMPOUND SENTENCE

☆ A compound sentence = two or more simple sentences joined by words like *and, but, or, nor, yet, for.*

☆ **Models**

1. Arthur invests in General Motors, and Christopher invests in Ford Motor.

2. America does well in world markets, but Japan offers serious competition.

3. The board has to humor the chairman, or he may retire earlier than planned.

4. I won't go to the conference, nor will I send an alternate.

5. Terence did not receive the promotion, yet I know that he deserves it.

6. Duncan's report went well, for he had spent hours preparing it.

Activity for Sentence Pattern #11

☞   Use each of the following words in a compound sentence. See the Appendix for some models.

   1. and

   2. but

   3. or

4. nor

5. yet

6. but

STAGE 9 WRAP-UP

☆ Intrigued by this Stage 9 concept of moving your main idea to positions other than first? Maybe you even found a favorite structure to use as part of your style.

☆ If you can find time for more writing, try these suggestions:

  1. difficult people at work

  2. ways to spend an invigorating Sunday

  3. achievements that I have accomplished

  4. reasons that I recommend the product that I sell

  5. my three greatest assets that I would list on a personnel file

  6. outstanding mentors I have had

☆ Write your paragraph in one of the Stage 9 structures.

  + 1st Power last

  + 1st Power first and last

  + 1st Power anywhere

  + 1st Power implied

  + 1st Power signaled by Red-Alert Signal

☆ In each paragraph, use one of the four new Sentence Patterns: #8-#9-#10-#11.

CHECKLIST

1. Paragraph in the Stage 9 structures   ———

2. Use of Sentence Patterns #8-#9-#10-#11   ———

3. Elimination of *there*   ———

4. Elimination of *to be*   ———

5. Stage 9s in 30 minutes   ———

6. Grammar, spelling, punctuation   ———

7. Neatness and margins (important courtesy)   ———

8. Second opinion   ———

☆ The way that you use Sentence Patterns and the structure of your paragraphs show your individual style. You should feel proud as your writing personality emerges.

☆ You have done an excellent job of writing your way through 9/10 of the Power Writing program. You have just 1/10 to go. Moving into Stage 10, you will find pleasure in developing the single paragraph into multi-paragraph memos, letters, and reports.

*Those who have been once intoxicated with Power
can never willingly abandon it.
(Edmund Burke—1729-1797)*

> ## *You're a 10 in anybody's book!*

STAGE 10

MULTI-PARAGRAPHING
(30 minutes, twice a week)

STAGE 10. . .

☆ Introduces multi-paragraphing

☆ Presents three new Sentence Patterns

MULTI-PARAGRAPHING

☆ Words and phrases have Power as they relate to other
words and phrases (Stages 1 and 2). Sentences within a
paragraph have Power as they relate to each other
(Stages 3-9). The same goes for paragraphs (Stage 10).

☆ A paragraph consists of one or more sentences about
one idea. A paragraph may have any length, depending
on how much emphasis and attention you wish to give
it. In dialogue writing, paragraphs may have only one
word.

☆ To make the transition from the single paragraph to
multi-paragraphing, just paragraph a Stage 8 at the
1st Power sentence and at each of the 2nd Power
sentences. This will result in a four-paragraph memo,
letter or report of 1 2 2 2.

A STAGE 8 PARAGRAPHED

For three reasons Van Doekker's Dutch Touch Restaurants may qualify as the next giant in fast-food franchising.

First, the product, sold as Panwiches, capitalizes on local food prices, adapts to regional and ethnic tastes, and serves as snacks, main course or dessert. These advantages give the product a wide market.

Second, the business offers operational benefits. Food preparation requires a small kitchen and storage area, with no sophisticated equipment.

Third, the franchiser, CutCo, has a history of innovating and replicating franchise successes. CutCo assists licensees in virtually every aspect of opening and operating.

How it works:

Not a word of the Stage 8, page 63, has changed to create this Stage 10. The Stage 10 has four paragraphs.

As a Stage 10, this becomes easier to read.

Stage 10 resembles *READER'S DIGEST* paragraphing.

STAGE 10 ACTIVITY 1

☞ Select any three of your Stage 8 paragraphs. Turn them into Stage 10s. Create four paragraphs: at the 1st Power sentence and at each of the 2nd Power sentences.

SENTENCE PATTERNS 12—13—14

12. Open a sentence with a gerund.
    (the "ing" form of the verb: *speaking*)

13. Use a clause that adds to the meaning.

14. Use a clause that can be deleted.

SENTENCE PATTERN # 12:
OPEN A SENTENCE WITH A GERUND

☆ The gerund = the "ing" form of the verb (writing, communicating, changing).

☆ **Models**

1. Sitting in afternoon meetings can become dull.

2. Changing company policies highlighted the session.

3. Writing effective letters requires precision.

4. Asking good questions reflects a keen mind.

5. Communicating in a large corporation often becomes a serious problem.

6. Reducing the budget focused upon military expenditures.

Activity for Sentence Pattern # 12

☞ Complete the following gerund openers. See the Appendix for samples.

    1. going

    2. arriving

3. calculating

4. competing

5. studying

6. accumulating

SENTENCE PATTERN # 13:
USE A CLAUSE THAT ADDS TO THE MEANING

☆ Only five words serve as openers for these clauses:
who, whom, which, that, whose.

☆ *Who, whom*, and *whose* refer to persons.

☆ *Which* and *that* refer to things.

☆ This type of clause does not take commas.

☆ **Models** (with the clauses in italics):

1. The people *who give form to mass-produced products*
   have fallen into a visual habit of cubic shapes, chrome
   trim, and dark-tinted plexiglass to solve all imaginable
   design dilemmas.
   (The *who* clause gives added meaning to *people*.)

2. Corporations *that own hotels, restaurants, and nightclubs
   hire for a broad spectrum of jobs.*
   (The *that* clause gives added meaning to *corporations*.)

3. Those *who want the government to help rejuvenate industries* often claim that the recovery of single companies would help the entire industry.
(The *who* clause specifies *those*. The *that* clause does not illustrate this Pattern.)

4. Companies *that accumulate cash and provide for adequate liquidity* have the best chances of survival.
(The *that* clause adds meaning to *companies*.)

5. Employers *who want to improve their protection against theft* can bring in security consultants, or they can do something about it themselves.
(The *who* clause explains *employers*.)

6. The technology *to which I refer* goes under various names.
(The *which* explains *technology*.)

Activity for Sentence Pattern # 13

☞   Complete the following so that they contain clauses that add to the meaning. See the Appendix for samples.

1. The person who

2. The man whom

3. The company that

4. All of the products that

5. The executives whose

6. The stocks and bonds that

SENTENCE PATTERN # 14:
USE A CLAUSE THAT CAN BE DELETED

☆ This kind of clause adds interest and detail to a sentence, but it is not essential.

☆ Four words serve as openers for these clauses: *who, whom, whose, which. Who, whom,* and *whose* refer to persons. *Which* refers to things. The word *that* cannot introduce this kind of clause.

☆ These clauses require commas.

☆ **Models** (with the clauses in *italics*)

1. The dial-a-panda service forms one of the most successful of the Nippon Telegraph and Telephone Company's array of information and entertainment recordings, *which constitute an integral part of its wide-ranging campaign to encourage the Japanese to use their telephones more often.*
   (*Which* refers to *recordings.*)

2. The board chairman, *whom many critics blasted,* continued his former policies.
   (*Whom* refers to *chairman.*)

3. Many people sought out Aristotle, *whose wisdom spread through the ancient world.*
   (*Whose* refers to *Aristotle.*)

4. Morgan Harris, *who will report directly to you,* will serve as Hadley's assistant.
   (*Who* refers to *Harris.*)

5. The audience applauded the speaker, *whose wit never faltered.*
   (*Whose* refers to *speaker.*)

6. In Greece, company executives can stay in "traditional settlements," *which lie far from the hubbub of cities like Athens.*
   (*Which* refers to *settlements.*)

Activity for Sentence Pattern # 14

☞ Complete the following clause openers. See the
   Appendix for samples.

   1. President Reagan, who

   2. The shareholders applauded the CEO's speech,
      which

   3. The attorney, whom

   4. Bertha Harris, whose

   5. The Republican Party, which

   6. Donald Trump, who

STAGE 10 MODELS

1.   In reply to your request for a recommendation for Marian Doubleday to act as a receptionist in your office, I can heartily praise her for three main reasons.

First, because of her gracious manner, she works well with all types of people. With tact and diplomacy, she has repeatedly handled our most difficult situations in the complaint department.

In addition to a pleasant attitude, she has a well-modulated telephone voice. Firm but flexible, her voice radiates a warm strength.

Furthermore, Mrs. Doubleday, who once worked as a reporter, has developed into a competent typist. Her typing speed exceeds sixty words per minute, with no errors.

This short essay of four paragraphs makes for fast, understandable reading. The first paragraph states "three reasons." The other three paragraphs open with 2nd Power links, to make finding the "three reasons" easy for the reader.

14
This clause, opening with *who*, provides additional information not really vital to the meaning of the sentence.

2. Our company has put together a special package, Superfit, to start you on the road to fitness.

    In just one hour a day for three days a week, this program will get you in shape. Superfit will enable you to firm up all those flabby muscles that you thought would always look soft.

    Second, if you start this weight-training program now, you can continue exercising to whatever age you choose. Dr. Leonard Goldman of the Olympic Training Center stated, "Weight training has proven safe and effective for people of all ages."

    Finally, we can offer you the Superfit package, which includes two sets of dumbbells and a total exercise program, for the unbelievably low price of $34.50. Working out for a month at your average health club would cost more than this total package.

At this Stage, do not try to apply Power to individual sentences. Paragraphs now have Power as they relate to each other.

13
That, which refers to *muscles,* introduces a clause vital to the meaning.

14
Which opens a clause not vital to the meaning.

12
Working is a gerund.

3. Warren Bennis, a business professor at the University of Southern California, has identified five qualities that successful chief executive officers must have. From least to most important, Bennis lists technical competence, people skills, conceptual skills, judgment, and character.

   Technical competence combines knowledge, broad experience, and the ability to do whatever one does as well as one can do. Technically competent executives have, more often than not, risen through the ranks and have some practical knowledge of and experience in nearly every aspect of their fields. They are smart, insatiably curious, and tireless workers.

   People skills include an understanding of oneself, talents and flaws alike, along with the ability to eliminate flaws or to compensate for them. People skills also require the capacity to understand and work with others as well as a gift for defining and expressing common needs. The executive who has such skills not only recognizes but enjoys the collaborative nature of business.

13
That **refers to** *qualities* **and opens a clause vital to the meaning.**

This essay, which has five 2nd Power paragraphs, shows that you don't have to restrict yourself to three points. Power helps you write anything you wish to write.

This writer lists the five qualities in the first paragraph. Then he discusses them one at a time, in order, in successive paragraphs.

13
Who **starts a clause vital to the meaning.**

Conceptual skills manifest themselves in an executive's viewpoint and vision. Successful executives enter their chosen field because they have a concrete notion of the world and what they want to make of it. That viewpoint, more than ambition, motivates them. As they rise, their viewpoint blossoms into a vision of what can and should be. Equipped with such vision, the able executive capitalizes on existing opportunities and anticipates future ones.

Clauses have subjects and verbs but cannot make sense alone.

Judgment, harder to measure than the first three qualities, proves a lot harder to come by. Blending that artful mix of brains and heart translates into understanding and steadiness. Leaders with judgment see and understand what's happening and respond decisively and intelligently. They don't overreact or go off half-cocked. At the same time, they act immediately, rather than leave it to fate or someone else.

12
***Blending* is a gerund. Gerunds are always used as nouns. *Blending* is the subject of the sentence.**

Everyone talks about character these days, and we claim to long for it in executive suites. But we have trouble defining it. Bennis's definition of character includes ambition, ability, and conscience in perfect order. A leader without character presents a contradiction in terms. Executives with character don't only do things right. They do the right thing and take full responsibility for their own actions and the actions of their organizations.

4. Since 1980, Donald Trump has become New York's most visible and extravagant real estate man, plastering his name over Manhattan Island like the label on a pair of designer jeans.

    In his first high-profile deal, he acquired the decrepit Commodore Hotel, hard by Grand Central Station and at the center of a neighborhood that, in the fiscal crisis year of 1975, had become shamefully run down. Trump sheathed the granite hotel in a new skin of green glass, reached a management arrangement with Hyatt Hotels, and reopened the building in 1980 as the Grand Hyatt.

    Soon after that, Trump built the Trump Tower. On Fifth Avenue, Trump Tower, which has glittering brass appointments and a pink marble retail lobby, has long since replaced the staid marble mansions and apartment houses a few blocks farther uptown as the popular symbol of luxury living. Nestled in a corner spot on Fifth Avenue next door to Tiffany's, Trump Tower condominiums sell for as much as 25% more than equivalent units in other high-grade midtown buildings.

    Across town, Trump Plaza has helped convert the Upper East Side from a neighborhood of townhouses and middle-class apartment blocks into an overbuilt community of high-rise *pieds-à-terre*.

    Trump has had close to a decade of experience in turning expectations and promotion into hard profits. Some Trump followers speculate that he may make a jump to the West Coast. With his increased holdings in MCA, he may have his eyes on MCA's generous holdings of real estate in Southern California.

How does this essay differ from other Stage 10s?

This essay has an opening, or 1st Power, paragraph. Then three paragraphs follow. Each discusses a Trump building. The essay closes with a 1st Power paragraph that ties everything together.

14
The *which* introduces interesting but non-vital material.

5.   The modern corporation has
four levels of personnel: the chief
executive, "middle management,"
tens of thousands of workers, and
"Bud."

At the top you will find a chief
executive, who spends his day
posing for Annual Report
photographs and testifying before
Congress.

Beneath him you will find
several thousand executives
engaged in "middle management."
This corporate term covers
"management activities in which
no one can possibly tell that
you've fouled up."

Beneath that second group you
will find tens of thousands of
secretarial, clerical, and reception
personnel.

At the bottom, somewhere in a
factory that nobody ever goes to
because it has no decent place
around it where you can have
lunch, you have the actual
production work force. This
consists of a grizzled old veteran
employee named "Bud."

Who **starts a clause
that has interesting
but non-vital
information.**

**What about the
structure of the Stage
10 essay?**

**This essay puts the
"four levels" into the
first paragraph. Each
successive paragraph
explains each level.
Thus, we have an
Essay of 1 2 2 2 2.**

STAGE 10: ACTIVITY 2

☞   Stage 8 contains other models that you have not yet
paragraphed. Select at least three of those to
paragraph as Stage 10s. In each, include one of the
three new Sentence Patterns: #12-#13-#14.

STAGE 10 WRAP-UP

☆ Although Stage 10 marks the end of the formal program, it also heralds the beginning of your new approach to writing, one in which you can incorporate the skills you have acquired.

☆ Using the following suggestions—or topics of your own choosing—write at least three Stage 10s. Include one of the new sentence patterns in each.

1. ways of improving the work environment

2. solutions to a city's traffic problems

3. kinds of information found in *The Wall Street Journal*

4. comparisons or contrasts of the U.S. dollar with foreign currencies

5. comparisons or contrasts of three cars with respect to gas economy

6. effects of inflation on people with fixed incomes

CHECKLIST

1. Stage 10 structure   ___

2. Use of Sentence Patterns #12-#13-#14   ___

3. Elimination of *there*   ___

4. Elimination of *to be*   ___

5. Stage 10 in 30 minutes   ___

6. Complete sentences   ___

7. Grammar, spelling, punctuation   ___

8. Neatness and margins (important courtesy)   ___

9. Second opinion   ___

☆ Congratulations upon finishing your Stage 10s!

☆ You must feel good about how far you have come from Stage 1 and how well you have done. Take a cooler break and savor the feeling!

☆ Read the Wrap-Up for the entire book.

WRAP-UP FOR THE BOOK

☆ Do you feel like a Power Writer by now? Frame some of your favorite writings. Hang them on the wall in your den. Then split a magnum of champagne with your editor!

☆ In a number of weeks or months you have gone from 3rd Power words to four-paragraph memos, letters, and reports. You have excellent control of Power at this point.

☆ Return to any of the 10 Stages you feel needs some extra attention.

☆ Have you noted the value of Power links and Red-Alert Signals, especially as your writing assignments lengthened? Can you see how much easier the reading became?

☆ Have you noticed how use of the Sentence Patterns strengthened the points you wished to make?

☆ As you find time, go to the Appendix for. . .

+ Elaboration and further explanation of points made at the 10 Stages

+ Methods of writing beyond Stage 10

+ More Sentence Patterns, with grammatical explanations

+ Infinite Power!

POST-TEST FOR POWER WRITERS

Now that you've completed the entire program, let's see how well you've learned all the skills. Choose a topic with which you are familiar on your job or use any of the topics provided in this book. Write a Stage 10 letter or memo. Use all of the following items, and ask a friend to edit your work:

☆ A clearly stated Power 1 (topic) sentence

☆ Power 2 and Power 3 sentences (major and minor details that support the topic sentence)

☆ Appropriate transitions

☆ No sentences starting with "there"

☆ No sentences using the verb "to be"

☆ A variety of sentence patterns

☆ A closing sentence that forwards an action

☆ Correct punctuation and grammar

☆ Correct spelling

By now, you have become a good judge of your own writing. Notice that your writing has developed a sense of flair and style. As in the pre-test, you may send us your paragraph for a final critique.

APPENDIX
STAGE 1

FROM THE PLAN TO THE PARAGRAPH

Before you begin to write, you must have the ideas to shape the message you want to convey. This will help you to think about your main idea as well as the details you need to support it. How you put your ideas together depends upon the audience you are addressing and the purpose of your writing. Develop an outline in which you list the points you want to make under the 1st Power word. You should list the points in sequence from most important to least important. Once you have the outline, all that you need are an introduction and conclusion.

POSSIBLE RESPONSES FOR STAGE 1 ACTIVITY

(1) hotels
> (2) Hilton
> (2) Marriott

(1) products
> (2) computers
> (2) calculators

(1) cities
> (2) Washington
> (2) London

(1) foods
        (2) meat
        (2) cheese

(1) Presidents
        (2) Hoover
        (2) Reagan

(1) stores
        (2) J. C. Penney
        (2) Sears

(1) resources
        (2) oil
        (2) gas

(1) countries
        (2) Sweden
        (2) France

(1) sports
        (2) football
        (2) tennis

(1) corporations
        (2) General Motors
        (2) Ford

STAGE 2

Moving your words into phrases will help you make your points more specific and focused. Although not as important as nouns and verbs, adjective phrases give your writing a vividness and style all its own. Practice turning sets of 1 2 2 word groups into 1 2 2 phrase groups. Avoid using phrases that are redundant or wordy.

POSSIBLE RESPONSES FOR STAGE 2 ACTIVITY

(1) hotel chains
      (2) Holiday Inn
      (2) Ramada Inn

(1) department stores
      (2) J.C. Penney
      (2) Neiman-Marcus

(1) electronic products
      (2) IBM computer
      (2) Canon copier

(1) natural resources
      (2) natural gas
      (2) mountain streams

(1) American cities
      (2) New York
      (2) New Orleans

(1) world nations
> (2) South Africa
> (2) New Zealand

(1) international foods
> (2) Swiss chocolate
> (2) Hungarian goulash

(1) sports leagues
> (2) NFL football
> (2) NBA basketball

FRAGMENTS MADE WHOLE

1. state-of-the-art programs
   IBM has announced state-of-the-art programs with its new computer line.

2. at the ticket office
   The secretary stopped at the ticket office to pick up passes for her boss.

3. two reasons for improving my writing
   I can cite two reasons for improving my writing.

4. to write this letter of complaint
   My dissatisfaction with your product forced me to write this letter of complaint.

STAGE 3

As you move into writing three-sentence paragraphs, notice how organizational problems disappear with the Power format.

The 1st Power sentence serves as a guide to your outline and unlocks the supporting details.

Keep your reader's attention by opening with a specific 1st Power sentence. Use the models throughout the book as guidelines to create your own 1st Power sentences when you reach Stage 4. Notice that the 1st Power sentence clearly states the main point to help the reader to stay focused. It is immediately followed with details to support the main idea. Although most of the models in the book have 1st Power sentences at the beginning of a paragraph, they may occur at the end or in some cases be implied.

CONCISENESS

Be concise. Eliminate all unnecessary words and sentences. Do not say any more than is absolutely necessary to communicate your message.

AVOID WORDY PHRASES

Wordy	*Simple and Clear*
for the purpose of	*to*
during periods when	*when*
by means of	*by*
due to the fact that	*because*
with reference to	*regarding / about*
make inquiry regarding	*ask*
in conjunction with	*with*
in the immediate future	*soon*
at the present time	*now / currently*
in view of the fact that	*because / since*

AVOID STILTED LANGUAGE

Stilted	*Specific*
endeavor	try
facilitate	ease
substantiate	explain/support
optimum	best
habitual	frequent
expeditious	fast/quick
remuneration	payment
procure	get
cognizant	aware

AVOID SEX-MARKED WORDS

Sexism	*Change to*
chairman	chairperson
salesman	sales agent
draftsman	drafter
he/she	job title
policeman	police officer
newsman	newscaster

AVOID REPETITIONS

Redundant	*Change to*
cut down	cut
in the neighborhood of	about
in view of the fact	because/since
consensus of opinion	consensus
at that time	then
final decision	decision
give consideration to	consider
in order to	to
it is thus clear	clearly
very unique	unique

SENTENCE LENGTH

Typical sentences in business should run between 12 and 20 words, but a 5- or 6-word sentence is often more forceful. Keep sentences short. Always work toward brevity and simplicity. Never be afraid to cut. As a general rule, you should have only one idea to develop in each sentence.

1. *Weak*: The law firm has taken a very favorable posture in relation to hiring a new partner.

   Strong: The law firm wants to hire a new partner.

2. *Weak*: I heard a rumor to the effect that his job was terminated.

   Strong: I heard a rumor that the company fired him.

3. *Weak*: In conclusion, it is my opinion that he, in fact, did not tell the truth about the contract.

   Strong: I believe he lied about the contract.

4. *Weak*: The sales agent engaged in a discussion about viable alternatives.

   Strong: The sales agent talked about possible solutions.

5. *Weak*: It is the consensus of opinion that the new innovation that we began using in January has created a huge difference in decreasing our cash deficit.

   Strong: Thank you again for the opportunity to develop systems that mutually benefit our companies.

YOUR AUDIENCE

Keep in mind the interests of your readers. Use the pronoun "you" to make the tone personal. Avoid stilted and formal language that tries to impress rather than express.

1. *Weak*: With a view to expanding the individual's knowledge of the Dun and Bradstreet's organization, operations, and service, members of the staff are periodically chosen for accelerated training. These programs give individuals a unique opportunity.

2. *Strong*: We would like to help you add to your training and also to know the company better. Our training will give you a unique opportunity.

TONE

Use words that promote a pleasant feeling. Remember that you are trying to create goodwill.

Negative	*Positive*
you failed to tell us	perhaps you overlooked
we are at a loss to understand	would you please explain
you can't	you need to
the regulations state	we ask that
you must	we request that

STAGE 4

1. In Stage 4, you start writing your own 1 2 2 paragraphs, in which you create 1st Power sentences. Remember that you want to capture the reader's interest and make an impact. Don't bury the main idea in the middle of the paragraph. Continue to use the models in this book for reference. You will notice that the examples lead with the main idea, although the 1st Power idea does not necessarily have to begin the paragraph.

2. In Stage 4, you will now use transitions, or links, to help the reader move from one sentence to another more smoothly. These words and phrases will make your writing easier to follow. Use this expanded list of 2nd Power links.

a key	*immediately*	*similarly*
a major	*in addition*	*soon*
as a result	*in spite of*	*specifically*
at length	*in the first place*	*the least*
at the same time	*in the second place*	*the most*
equally important	*initially*	*then*
finally	*next*	*therefore*
first	*on the other hand*	*to conclude*
for example	*once*	*today*
for instance	*second*	*unfortunately*

3. EDITING: Before moving on to Stage 5, get help from someone else who can criticize your writing objectively. Most of us do a terrible job of proofreading our own correspondence because we have become too emotionally involved in the content. Have your writings read for sentence flow and accuracy.

4. SPELLING: Always keep a good dictionary at your side. The *American Heritage Dictionary* and *Webster's New World Dictionary* are excellent. *Webster's Instant Word Guide*, another fine resource, lists 35,000 words syllabically.

POSSIBLE RESPONSES FOR STAGE 4 ACTIVITY 1

1. In two ways I enjoy my job with Pacific Bell.

2. Two motion pictures—*Wall Street* and *Executive Suite*—illustrate negative as well as positive aspects of the business world.

3. When I take a client to lunch, I make reservations at either Perino's or the Occidental Tower.

4. After reaching the convention center, Roger checked the seminar program for two worthwhile sessions.

5. Small businesses offer two advantages.

6. On the way to my desk at the office, I pass two grating personalities.

7. Everyday I see "games" being played on the job.

STAGE 5

You have now expanded paragraphs from three sentences to five sentences, adding a minor detail to each major detail. Once you have reached Stage 5, you will figure out how to get to 4th and 5th and other Powers. You will also observe that your writing will not automatically follow a 1 2 3 2 3 pattern. It could follow a 1 2 2 2 2 pattern, a 1 2 2 3 3 pattern or any pattern you wish. We started with the structure of 1 2 3 2 3 to eliminate fundamental errors before they became ingrained.

Continue to practice eliminating the word "there" from the beginnings of all your sentences. This technique will make your sentences stronger and less wordy.

POSSIBLE RESPONSES FOR ACTIVITY FOR ELIMINATION OF *THERE*

1. I have several key responsibilities as program manager.

2. I have found several lovely places to vacation.

3. You should invest in AT & T for several reasons.

4. In my career, I have had interesting on-the-job experiences.

5. My product line has two special features which benefit consumers.

STAGE 6

Notice that throughout this book we have made every effort to de-emphasize weak verbs, so that you see examples of more persuasive correspondence.

Continue to think of new ways to structure your own sentences to eliminate forms of the verb *to be*. If possible, read your sentences aloud to a friend so that you will hear the difference between passive verbs and strong action verbs. Soon your writing will take on greater clarity and precision.

Use some of the following strong verbs in your business writing:

administer	*generate*	*provide*
analyze	*implement*	*realize*
coordinate	*increase*	*research*
create	*neglect*	*reduce*
develop	*present*	*structure*
direct	*produce*	*write*

POSSIBLE RESPONSES FOR THE ACTIVITY FOR *TO BE*

1. Under the new tax law, employers should make more accurate withholding.

2. To qualify for a refund, I must file a return.

3. Certain individuals do not qualify for the standard deduction.

4. This rule took effect for the 1985 tax year.

5. Two worksheets appear on the back of the form.

6. The income tax rate for individuals on net capital gains will not exceed 28%.

7. The old edition of the tax book went out of use in 1986.

8. Warner will not change his stand against higher taxes.

POSSIBLE RESPONSES FOR ACTIVITIES FOR STRONG ACTION VERBS

1. Simon *managed* his accounting division with ruthless efficiency.

2. The sales manager *gave* the new staff an intensive orientation.

3. The huge federal deficit *fuels* the fires of inflation.

4. The secretary's telemarketing skills greatly *increased* company profits.

5. The personnel director *hired* more employees with knowledge of high technology and hands-on experience.

6. The company will *expand* overseas operations.

STAGE 7

Observe how frequently you begin sentences with the same subject-verb word order. Although much of business writing often follows that format, using a wide variety of sentence patterns will give your writing more flair and personal identity. If you see yourself falling into a rut with the same pattern, create new sentence variations to eliminate the monotony.

POSSIBLE RESPONSES FOR SENTENCE PATTERN # 1 ACTIVITY

1. Critics *rave* about the sports facilities at the Seoul Olympics.

2. The treasurer *proposed* a more restrictive policy regarding executive travel.

3. Factory workers at many companies have *received* incentive bonuses to increase production.

4. The department chairman *fired* two staff members for excessive absences.

5. The chairman of the board *asked* the vice president to research declining sales figures.

6. Cellular telephones have *revolutionized* communications for executives who must tackle the freeways.

POSSIBLE RESPONSES FOR SENTENCE PATTERN # 2 ACTIVITY

1. Who determines the vacation schedule at Source Finders?

2. What negative effects have resulted from program trading?

3. When will the United States realize that massive military budgets have created an overall economic decline?

4. Where should the company have its convention?

5. Why has Ford outdistanced its American competitors in the automobile industry?

6. How do General Motors and Ford differ in wages?

POSSIBILE RESPONSES FOR SENTENCE PATTERN # 3 ACTIVITY

1. Soon, a new portable television with a built-in VCR will arrive on the market.

2. Sharply, the chairman of the Presidential AIDS Commission challenged Reagan for failing to take strong action against the disease.

3. Today, the president will make announcements that will affect the future of Q.E.D. Publications.

4. Desperately, the Government of Korea has pressured Hyundai to resolve its labor problems.

5. Temporarily, company headquarters will move to Pittsburgh.

6. Recently, *Consumer Reports* criticized the new Suzuki Samurai as "not acceptable."

POSSIBLE RESPONSES FOR SENTENCE PATTERN # 4 ACTIVITY

1. Despite the Soviet scandal, Toshiba's profits continue to soar.

2. Through the efforts of the sales staff, the company showed a profit in 1988.

3. In an effort to improve staff morale, the company reimbursed staff members who attended the sales seminars.

4. Within the year, the company will make changes in its marketing policies.

5. In spite of adversity, Hugh emerged as the victor in the lawsuit.

6. Without capable leadership, a business will often lose its competitive edge.

STAGE 8

PARAGRAPH LENGTH: As you see your paragraphs expanding to seven sentences, you may grow uneasy and want to start a new paragraph. Although there is no rule specifying the number of sentences a paragraph should contain, do not overwhelm the writer with lengthy paragraphs. Always be sensitive to keeping paragraphs short.

POSSIBLE MODELS FOR SENTENCE PATTERN # 5 ACTIVITY

1. Lee Iacocca, chairman of the board of Chrysler Corporation, has written a best-selling biography.
2. General Motors, the largest American car manufacturer, has joined with Japan on a car-making venture.
3. Sanyo, a firm that makes a variety of audio-visual equipment, has remained competitive in the high-tech marketplace.
4. The board decided to hold its March meeting in Atlanta, site of its 1989 convention.
5. Donald Trump, the astounding New York entrepreneur, has written a compelling biography.
6. Japan, one of our closest allies, causes much concern in economic circles with its restrictive trade policies.

POSSIBLE MODELS FOR SENTENCE PATTERN # 6 ACTIVITY

1. Because the company had high quarterly profits, the board voted a bonus to the workers.
2. Although Donald Trump has experienced much success, he has harsh critics of his policies.
3. Whenever anyone questions the publisher about editorial policies, he politely changes the subject.
4. Until the new staff arrived, the company continued to show uneven quality of its products and delays in their delivery.

5. Though many workers expected an immediate explanation, the chairman of the board did give advance notice of the plant closing.

6. When companies start improving quality and reducing inventories, the economy will once again boom.

POSSIBLE MODELS FOR SENTENCE PATTERN # 7 ACTIVITY

1. Los Angeles, New York, and London have main branches of the Bank of America.

2. General Motors, Ford Motor Company, and Chrysler Motors constitute the Big Three of American auto-making.

3. Lee Iacocca, Donald Trump, and Carl Icahn constantly make front-page news in business and other publications.

4. Products from Beatrice go to the farm, to the factory, and to the home.

5. Wherever I have gone, wherever I go, and wherever I will go, people remember my films.

6. I offer my resignation with regret at leaving, with appreciation for all you have done, and with hope that the organization might miss me.

STAGE 9

BEGINNINGS AND CLOSINGS

In some correspondence you may not want to hit the reader with the main idea first; rather, you may wish to begin with a hook or an attention-getter that makes one desire to read further. We call these introductory or background sentences Zero Power. They should heighten the readers' interest so that readers pay attention to your message.

When writing a letter, avoid old-fashioned "boilerplate" beginnings.

Old-Fashioned	*Fresh*
this is in reference to	thank you for your letter
enclosed please find	I have included
to whom it may concern	Dear Mr./Ms.
pursuant to your memo of	as a follow-up to your memo
it is with deepest regret	we regret
we herewith request	we ask that

Much business correspondence requires a closing statement to forward an action requested. Include closures whenever you wish. Keep those closing statements short and friendly. Good closures should tell the reader what you want done to what action you will take.

Weak	*Strong*
hoping to hear from you soon	Please answer our letter by October 22.
It has been a pleasure to be of assistance to you.	I enjoyed working with you.
Please feel free to call.	Please call.
Let us state again in closing	To conclude,
This is to acknowledge receipt of your contribution.	Thank you for your generous gift.

If you concur, please let me know.

I'll call you next Monday to discuss the issue.

POSSIBLE RESPONSES FOR SENTENCE PATTERN # 8 ACTIVITY

1. To understand the company's financial crisis, I need to have the details.

2. To do the job better and faster, the workers will need technological know-how.

3. To finance the factory equipment, the board will need a large bank loan.

4. To attend the committee meeting, the members will have to travel by air.

5. To have fluency in Spanish will become a necessary requirement for many managers in the future.

6. To negotiate, the union will need to know the company's offer.

POSSIBLE RESPONSES FOR SENTENCE PATTERN # 9 ACTIVITY

1. Failing to remain solvent, the nation's thrift and loans need help from Congress.

2. Reacting to sanctions against South Africa, many companies have found ways to do business by dealing with neighbor nations.

3. Signing the contract for the computer lease, Ron immediately realized how it would streamline the entire office operation.

4. Sitting alone in Sheraton's executive conference room, Randall decided to install full-service health clubs in all the hotels.

5. Judging the current economic indicators, the investors had concerns about inflation.

6. Finding the information he needed about company health insurance, Woody incorporated it into his notes.

POSSIBLE RESPONSES FOR SENTENCE PATTERN # 10 ACTIVITY

1. Driven with ambition, Hank sought the presidency of the company.

2. Renovated four years ago, the company dining room already shows signs of deterioration.

3. Persuaded by the chairman, the board voted in favor of the resolution to restrict executive travel perks.

4. Based on recent sales, the manager will make changes in consumer operations.

5. Bypassed in office promotions, Alderson decided to seek another job.

6. Promised the next vice-presidency, Harry started solidifying his position with the board members.

POSSIBLE RESPONSES FOR SENTENCE PATTERN # 11 ACTIVITY

1. Jack works at McDonald's, and his brother Sam works at Wendy's.

2. Morgan earns a fair salary, but his counterpart at a rival firm earns almost twice as much.

3. The manager will have to give Janice a raise, or she may seek another position.

4. Jim will not make a bid, nor will he even consider one.

5. Sullivan did not make a strong defense of his position, yet I know that he had prepared himself thoroughly.

6. Drake's suggestions about insurance investments received wide acceptance, but his speeches turned people off.

STAGE 10

Your writing has now moved from a single paragraph to a multi-paragraphed memo or letter. By simply paragraphing at each of the 1st and 2nd Power sentences, you have now created a document that the reader can quickly and easily follow.

THE FINAL DRAFT

Now is when you make certain that your reader understands you. Read your rough draft several times. Refer to all of the EDITING standards introduced in Stages 1-10.

Check the Organization:

❏ Did you introduce the subject clearly with a specific topic sentence?

❏ Did you include specific details sufficient for the topic?

❏ Did you arrange the sentences in logical order?

❏ Does your closing sentence forward the action?

Check for Readability and Sentence Flow:

❏ Are your sentences too long?

❏ Did you proofread for complete sentences?

❏ Does your choice of words assume too much or too little about the reader?

Check for a Personal Tone:

❏ Did you use positive language?

❏ Did you consider the sensitivity of your reader?

❏ Did you substitute "we" and "you" wherever possible?

Check Grammar, Spelling, and Punctuation:

❏ Did you use subject-verb agreement?

❏ Did you use proper tenses?

❑ Did you check to see that your writing is free of spelling errors?

❑ Did you use commas, hyphens, and apostrophes correctly?

REMEMBER THAT TWO EDITORS ARE BETTER THAN ONE!

POSSIBLE RESPONSES FOR SENTENCE PATTERN # 12 ACTIVITY

1. Going to committee meetings can occupy too much time.

2. Arriving at work on time impresses the boss.

3. Calculating monthly statistics keeps one clerk busy.

4. Competing against rivals proves stimulating.

5. Studying financial reports can fill hours.

6. Accumulating business knowledge helps me better understand operations.

POSSIBLE RESPONSES FOR SENTENCE PATTERN # 13 ACTIVITY

1. The person who does the best job on the assembly line will receive extra compensation.

2. The man whom the office staff highly respected represented a person with high standards.

3. The company that provides the best advertising program will probably make the highest sales.

4. All of the products that IBM manufactures have exceptional quality.

5. The executive whose ideas show future promise will probably become the next CEO.

6. The stocks and bonds that show the greatest short-term earnings will appeal to some clients.

POSSIBLE RESPONSES FOR SENTENCE PATTERN # 14 ACTIVITY

1. President Reagan, who conducted one of his rare press conferences, made an astounding announcement.

2. The shareholders applauded the CEO's speech, which set up plans for future growth.

3. The attorney, whom the company had chosen from a large list, represented his clients well.

4. Bertha Harris, whose company enjoys large profits, showed that a woman can succeed in the male-dominated construction industry.

5. The Republican Party, which nominated Dewey, did not realize the impact of Truman.

6. Donald Trump, who makes real estate headlines, has written an interesting biography.

A FIVE-PARAGRAPH PROFILE

The Donald Trump Profile in Stage 10 has five paragraphs—a 1st Power paragraph, three 2nd Power paragraphs, and a concluding 1st Power paragraph. That structure forms the organization of the five-paragraph profile.

The following five-paragraph profile retains much of the content of the Trump material as it appeared in Stage 10. The difference here lies in the longer length of each paragraph.

At this point in your writing, you can make paragraphs any length you desire to get your message across.

Donald Trump, son of an oldline builder of subsidized housing in the middle-class residential boroughs of Brooklyn and Queens, brought his father's real estate empire into Manhattan soon after graduating from Wharton School of Business in 1968. No one would claim that Trump would ever show weakness on self-promotion. Since 1980, Donald Trump has become New York's most *visible* and extravagant real estate man, plastering his name over Manhattan Island like the label on a pair of designer jeans.

This 1st Power paragraph contains the main idea: that Trump is a *visible* real estate man.

In his first high-profile deal, he acquired the decrepit Commodore Hotel,
hard by Grand Central Station and at
the center of a neighborhood that, in the
fiscal crisis year of 1975, had become
shamefully rundown. Trump sheathed
the granite hotel in a new skin of green
glass, reached a management arrangement with Hyatt Hotels, and reopened
the building in 1980 as the Grand
Hyatt. The hotel and the Grand Central
district experienced rebirth together at
the start of the fiscal revival of New
York in the 1980's.

This 2nd Power paragraph presents the Grand Hyatt, the first example of Trump's visibility.

Soon after the opening of the Grand
Hyatt, Trump built the Trump Tower.
On Fifth Avenue, Trump Tower, which
has glittering brass appointments and a
pink marble retail lobby, has long since
replaced the staid marble mansions and
apartment houses a few blocks farther
uptown as the popular symbol of luxury
living. Nestled in a corner spot on Fifth
Avenue next door to Tiffany's, Trump
Tower condominiums sell for as much as
25% more than equivalent units in other
high-grade mid-town buildings. Corporations and non-resident investors have
purchased 74% of the units.

This 2nd Power paragraph contains the second example of Trump's visibility: Trump Tower.

Meanwhile, across town in Manhattan,
Trump Plaza has helped convert the
upper East Side from a neighborhood of
townhouses and middle-class apartment
blocks into an overbuilt community of
high-rise *pieds-à-terre*.

This 2nd Power paragraph mentions Trump Plaza, the third example of Trump's visibility.

Trump has had close to a decade of experience in turning expectations and promotion into hard profits. Some Trump followers speculate that he may make a jump to the West Coast. With his increasing holdings in MCA, he may have his eyes on MCA's generous amounts of real estate in Southern California.*

This closing 1st Power paragraph ties the profile together with *decade of experience* **and a look into a possible future.**

AN EIGHT-PARAGRAPH PROFILE

To create an eight-paragraph profile, do not change a word of the previous five-paragraph profile. Just add a 3rd Power paragraph after each of the 2nd Power paragraphs. Now you will have a profile that consists of a 1st Power paragraph, three 2nd Power paragraphs, three 3rd Power paragraphs, and a concluding 1st Power paragraph.

At this point you can create a profile or report of any length. You can add 4th Power or other-Power paragraphs as your content dictates.

Donald Trump, son of an oldline builder of subsidized housing in the middle-class residential boroughs of Brooklyn and Queens, brought his father's real estate empire into Manhattan soon after graduating from Wharton School of Business in 1968. No one would claim that Trump would ever show weakness on self-promotion. Since 1980, Donald Trump has become New York's most visible and extravagant real estate man, plastering his name over Manhattan Island like the label of a pair of designer jeans.

This 1st Power paragraph identifies the main idea of the entire profile: that Trump has a *visible* **real estate presence.**

*Adapted from "N.Y.'s' Landlord' May Be Shopping on the West Coast," by Michael Hiltzik. Copyright © Feb. 28, 1988, *Los Angeles Times*. Reprinted by permission.

In his first high-profile deal, he acquired the decrepit Commodore Hotel, hard by Grand Central Station and at the center of a neighborhood that, in the fiscal crisis year of 1975, had become shamefully rundown. Trump sheathed the granite hotel in a new skin of green glass, reached a management arrangement with Hyatt Hotels, and reopened the building in 1980 as the Grand Hyatt. The hotel and the Grand Central district experienced rebirth together at the start of the fiscal revival of New York in the 1980's. However, Trump's ventures do embroil him in local disputes.

This 2nd Power paragraph contains the first example of Trump's "visible" presence: the Grand Hyatt Hotel.

Trump carries on a running feud with New York Mayor Edward I. Koch. The disagreement erupted over Trump's most grandiose proposal. He plans a 100-acre development on a Manhattan riverfront site. The feud between Trump and Koch centers upon Trump's plan to attract NBC from its Rockefeller Center location to the new site.

This 3rd Power paragraph makes the connection between *running feud* and *local disputes* in the 2nd Power paragraph.

Soon after the opening of the Grand Hyatt, Trump built the Trump Tower. On Fifth Avenue, Trump Tower, which has glittering brass appointments and a pink marble retail lobby, has long since replaced the staid marble mansions and apartment houses a few blocks farther uptown as the popular symbol of luxury living. Nestled in a corner spot on Fifth Avenue next door to Tiffany's, Trump Tower condominiums sell for as much as 25% more than equivalent units in other high-grade mid-town buildings. Corporations and non-resident investors have purchased 74% of the units.

This 2nd Power paragraph refers back to the Grand Hyatt to keep the reader on target.

Much as Trump made his name in Manhattan, he has truly made his mark in Atlantic City. He took a costly casino off the Hilton Hotels hands so fast that the Hilton name still appeared on the slot machines. Known as Trump's Castle today, its revenue growth has consistently remained among the top five of Atlantic City's twelve casinos.

This 3rd Power paragraph moves to Atlantic City from Trump's "visibility" in Manhattan.

Meanwhile, across town in Manhattan, Trump Plaza has helped convert the upper East Side from a neighborhood of townhouses and middle-class apartment blocks into an overbuilt community of high-rise *pieds-à-terre*.

Meanwhile **gets the reader back to Manhattan and the third example of Trump's "visibility" there: Trump Plaza.**

The other Trump Plaza—in Atlantic City—ranks as one of the gambling town's most heavily marketed and most successful casinos. Trump, former owner of the now defunct New Jersey Generals, has expressed an interest in the financially troubled New England Patriots.

Trump Plaza in Manhattan provides the transition to Trump Plaza in Atlantic City—and a 3rd Power paragraph.

Trump has had close to a decade of experience in turning expectations and promotion into hard profits. Some Trump followers speculate that he may make a jump to the West Coast. With his increasing holdings in MCA, he may have his eyes on MCA's generous amounts of real estate in Southern California.*

This concluding 1st Power paragraph makes reference to a decade of experience, which reinforces Trump's visibility

* Adapted from "N. Y.'s' Landlord' May Be Shopping on the West Coast," by Michael Hiltzik. Copyright © Feb. 28, 1988, *Los Angeles Times*. Reprinted by permission.

39 SENTENCE PATTERNS

The 10 Stages of this book introduced you to 14 Sentence Patterns. The authors have identified 39 such patterns. Once you feel comfortable using the 14 in the main text, study some of the other 25 and try to use some of them in future writing.

For each of the 39 patterns, one example appears.

1. USE STRONG ACTION VERBS.

   The financial problems perplexed the treasurer.

2. ASK A QUESTION.

   Why do factories establish rules for workers?

3. USE AN EXCLAMATORY SENTENCE.

   What incredible profits the company made in the last quarter!

4. OPEN A SENTENCE WITH AN ADVERB.

   Tomorrow the company will move its headquarters to Atlanta.

5. OPEN A SENTENCE WITH A PREPOSITIONAL PHRASE.

   In June 1988, the board implemented a new accounting system.

6. WRITE A SENTENCE IN WHICH THE VERB PRECEDES THE SUBJECT.

   Throughout the treasurer's report appear thinly disguised references to spending policies.

7. USE CONVERSATION OR A QUOTATION.

   Our advertising brochure comes to you "hot off the press."

8. USE APPOSITION.

   James Hartley, a dogged researcher, provided some thoughtful answers at the board meeting.

9. OPEN A SENTENCE WITH AN ADVERBIAL CLAUSE.

   Unless unexpected delays occur, the workers will finish the new wing by spring.

10. USE PARALLEL STRUCTURE IN WORDS, PHRASES, CLAUSES, AND SENTENCES.

The bank offers checking, savings, trust, leasing, and lending services.

11. OPEN A SENTENCE WITH AN ADJECTIVE.

Cheerful, Clark walked away from the meeting with pleasure at how well it had gone.

12. OPEN A SENTENCE WITH AN ADJECTIVAL PHRASE.

Confident at his newfound ability, Peter could write a memo on a moment's notice.

13. OPEN A SENTENCE WITH A PRESENT INFINITIVE.

To avoid other collection procedures, please send a check for $40.00 by August 31.

14. OPEN A SENTENCE WITH A PERFECT INFINITIVE.

To have spoken at the sales convention, I should have received an invitation.

15. OPEN A SENTENCE WITH A PRESENT PARTICIPLE.

Typewriting rapidly, the secretary finished the letter before going home.

16. OPEN A SENTENCE WITH A PAST PARTICIPLE.

Impressed by the speeches, the sales force left the hall eager to try out some of the ideas that had been introduced.

17. OPEN A SENTENCE WITH A PERFECT PARTICIPLE.

Having completed his report, Hall sat back to await reactions.

18. OPEN A SENTENCE WITH A DIRECT OBJECT.

Instant gratification the manager promised, if the workers would follow his suggestions.

19. OPEN A SENTENCE WITH A VERB.

Muttered Mason under his breath, "How do we handle this situation?"

20. OPEN A SENTENCE WITH A PRESENT GERUND.

Communicating with his colleagues poses a problem for Blanchard.

21. OPEN A SENTENCE WITH A PERFECT GERUND.

Without having had any previous experience, Meehan secured the position over other applicants.

22. USE A RESTRICTIVE ADJECTIVAL CLAUSE.

The idea that came to the chairman seemed brilliant.

23. USE A NON-RESTRICTIVE ADJECTIVAL CLAUSE.

All of our branches, which you will find throughout the city, have automated teller machines.

24. OPEN A SENTENCE WITH A NOUN CLAUSE.

Where we will hold the sales convention becomes a matter of compromise.

25. OPEN A SENTENCE WITH A PREDICATE NOUN.

An agreeable fellow the new assistant office manager seems.

26. OPEN A SENTENCE WITH A PREDICATE ADJECTIVE.

Angry the chairman seemed when he heard the news about the proposed merger.

27. WRITE A COMPOUND SENTENCE, USING A COMMA BEFORE SUCH CONJUNCTIONS AS *and, but, or, nor, yet, for*.

I rated the speaker highly, but I disliked the food.

28. WRITE A COMPOUND SENTENCE USING A SEMICOLON BUT NO CONJUNCTION.

I praised the speaker enthusiastically; I criticized the luncheon food strongly.

29. WRITE A COMPOUND SENTENCE USING THE SEMICOLON BEFORE COORDINATING CONJUNCTIONS (*and, but, or, nor, for, yet*) BECAUSE THE SENTENCE ALREADY CONTAINS COMMAS.

During the first half of October, the board chairman visited plants in Oshkosh, Ashtabula, and West Union; and just before the holidays, he traveled to Paducah, Parnassus, and Poughkeepsie.

30. WRITE A COMPOUND SENTENCE USING THE SEMICOLON BEFORE AND A COMMA AFTER SUCH CONNECTIVES AS *however, therefore, consequently, nevertheless, thus, in fact, then, on the other hand.*

The office manager has several weaknesses; however, he has many strong points, which make up for his weak ones.

31. WRITE A COMPOUND SENTENCE WITH ELLIPTICAL CONSTRUCTION.

Some reporters try to take down all the information at the company's press conferences; others, only the main points.

32. WRITE A COMPOUND SENTENCE WITH AN INTRODUCTORY, OR GENERAL, STATEMENT FOLLOWED BY A COLON AND A SPECIFIC, OR EXPLANATORY, STATEMENT.

Some fortunate parts of the country may not feel the recession at all: the Southwest and Intermountain West continue to surge because of high demand for their energy resources.

33. USE A PARENTHETICAL EXPRESSION BETWEEN THE SUBJECT AND THE VERB.

The new accounting system, in contrast with the old one, will save the company time and money.

34. OPEN A SENTENCE WITH AN INTRODUCTORY SERIES OF APPOSITIVES, WITH A DASH AND A SUMMARIZING SUBJECT.

Courtesy, correctness, conciseness—these constitute the three essentials of a business letter.

35. USE AN EMPHATIC APPOSITIVE AT THE END OF A SENTENCE, FOLLOWING A COLON.

    Adjusting to a new role as CEO requires one quality: the ability to laugh at oneself.

36. USE AN EMPHATIC APPOSITIVE AT THE END OF A SENTENCE, FOLLOWING A DASH.

    Now an even more miserable machine tyrannizes man's daily life—the computer.

37. USE AN INTERNAL SERIES OF APPOSITIVES OR MODIFIERS, ENCLOSED BY A PAIR OF DASHES.

    The necessary qualities for corporate life—guile, ruthlessness, and garrulity—the CEO learned by carefully studying his predecessors.

38. OPEN A SENTENCE WITH A NOMINATIVE ABSOLUTE.

    All things considered, the economy will return to normal.

39. USE A PERIODIC SENTENCE.

    If the workers exert efforts in the factory, if the resulting products have quality, and if the sales force does its job, the company will increase profits this quarter.

WHAT NEXT?

☆ After you have completed *Power Writing*, continue practicing your writing on a daily basis. Whenever you have 10 minutes, sit down to write something.

☆ Start talking about the importance of thinking and writing clearly to your manager, supervisors, and friends.

☆ Within your company, set up training programs that devote time to actual writing. Use samples drawn from your job as models for editing and possible revision.

☆ Establish a reward system for people who bring recognition to your company through powerful written communication.

☆ Let people within your company know that effective writing immediately brings positive recognition to your office image.

☆ Now that you have learned how to produce powerful memos, letters, and reports, start showing other professionals how to write persuasive and articulate sentences and paragraphs.

☆ Above all, give yourself a "big pat on the back" for developing literacy and clarity in your own writing. You have now mastered a skill that will bring you success and respect on the job and in other aspects of your life.